"Thank you very much for all your hard work for the community. The good food, friendships, and social meetings that everyone thrives on, socialising and eating meals together. You are all worth celebrating for your community work, bringing everyone together."

*Pantry member*

# SOUP for GOOD

Recipes and stories from the
Cook for Good community

Cook for Good is a social enterprise based in London's Kings Cross working to tackle food insecurity, social isolation, and barriers to work through a programme that includes free cooking classes, community meals, training and work experience, and a surplus food pantry. All profits from this book will be fed into the community programme.

First hardback edition published in 2024 by
Cook for Good Community Interest Company

www.cookforgood.uk

Copyright © Cook for Good, 2024


PHOTOGRAPHY

© Jason Boswell, 2024 (all recipe images)

© Martin Godwin, 2024 (pages 10, 13, 28, 31, 40, 43, 58, 61, 70, 73, 102, 105, 118, 121, 136, 139, 150, 153, 166, 169, 182, 185, 192, 195)

© Manuel Harlan, 2024 (pages 20, 44, 87, 90–91, 126, 162, 202–203)

© Justin Gardner, 2024 (page 6)

Book design, printing, and binding by PrintHouse Corporation.

Printed in the UK using vegetable-based inks onto materials from certified well-managed sources.


A CIP catalogue record for this book is available from the British Library

ISBN 978-1-3999-8286-3

FOREWORD                           5

INTRODUCTION                       7

A FEW TIPS AND TRICKS             14

THE MAGIC OF HOMEMADE STOCK       15

A WORLD OF CHICKEN SOUP           17

TWO WAYS WITH...                  45

USE IT UP                         83

A MEAL IN A BOWL                 127

TOPPING IT OFF                   161

NO STRESS BREADS                 175

INDEX                            196

ACKNOWLEDGEMENTS                 200

# FOREWORD

For me, soup sums up all that I love about cooking: it's adaptable, resourceful in its ability to turn bits and pieces into a meal that's sustaining, comforting and uplifting, and the possibilities and variety are boundless. Soup is universal and also preciously intimate: to offer a bowl or mug of soup to someone is an act of cosiness and connection. And that is exactly what Cook for Good offers: a bustling place where a community can come together and sustain each other. And I feel that this sense of mutual support is key to Cook for Good and what makes it such a vibrant and welcoming place. Those who come and shop or eat here are also invited to contribute. They can come and learn from visiting chefs, and they can teach how to cook their own food, too. Everyone has a story, and here is where they come to share it.

The lines Cook for Good runs on are egalitarian and respectful; its focus is the dignity of the individual and the community. It has been awe-inspiring to see it thrive and, in turn, create a thriving culture around it. This book expands its remit, expressing its essence and allowing all of us to be part of an endeavour that shows the enduring value of connection – as elemental to our wellbeing as the soups that are offered daily in Cook for Good's lively premises.

Nigella Lawson

*Karen Mattison and Robinne Collie, Co-Founders*

# INTRODUCTION

Like all the very best recipes, Cook for Good is the result of combining some simple ingredients to create something magical. It all started when we met back in 2019 and discovered that we shared a belief in the power of food to bring people and communities together.

As our conversations evolved, we started to think about trying something new. What would happen if we were able to get involved with a real community? How could we provide deep and lasting support for people in a time of hardship, with food and cooking as the way in? And could there be a way to do so alongside local businesses that shared our appetite for change?

Together, with the help of a growing team, we made plans to create a community kitchen and surplus food pantry on a housing estate. And in 2021, after a lot of searching and a few pandemic-related false starts, we set up home on the Peabody Priory Green Estate in Kings Cross, an area of huge investment which has largely passed the local community by.

We started by turning a disused laundry into a community pantry, co-run by community volunteers, where members pay £3.50 a week to choose a basket of surplus food worth around £35. We transformed a derelict café into a community kitchen, where residents aged between 5 and 85 can take part in free cooking classes and courses, such as the Men's Grub Club for older male residents and Cook for Health for diabetes patients. It's also where our Community Brigade programme trains local people to access jobs in catering and hospitality.

Today, Cook for Good is everything we hoped it would be and more. It is a beacon of hope, joy, and friendship serving the whole community, who have given us the warmest of welcomes. Though the real issues of food insecurity, social isolation, and barriers to employment persist, the community know we are here to stay – a commitment made possible by the generous support of our Peabody landlords, our teambuilding clients, and our community and corporate partners.

And the spaces we have created are more than just facilities: they are the beating heart of our community. They are where residents come together to cook, eat, shop, chat, and get advice, where neighbours who were strangers have now become friends. As one of them told us: "Without Cook for Good, we would not have the community we have now."

So why write a soup book? It all began one cold winter's day in 2022 when Karen brought in a flask of homemade soup and offered some to Mary, one of our volunteers. Mary enjoyed it so much that Karen took home some wonky leftover carrots and made enough carrot soup to share with all the volunteers the following week. Before long, our members were also asking for a taste, so we decided to add a soup café to our Pantry offering.

Since then, we have served soup to our members every single week. Some recipes came from old family recipes, handed down through generations; others were shared by our members and volunteers from their cultures and countries. Others were simply developed because we had surplus fennel or squash and wanted to show people how to use it.

We always offer two soups, believing that choice is the bedrock of dignity – although many members like to try both. Our pantry manager, Tom, always receives instant, frank feedback, which consigns some to the recipe dustbin, while others are requested time and again. And as our list of favourites grew, we saw a way to share the story of the soups we love, and the community who have become like family, with a wider audience.

*Soup for Good* tells that story. It's a celebration of soup: the simplest of meals with the power to change the world. After all, what do we turn to when we are unwell? Soup. How do we show love to those who are in need? Soup. Every culture has its own healing soups, and every family has their favourites. In our community, soup is quite literally the food that brings people together.

*Soup for Good* is also a celebration of our community: of the resilient, brilliant people of Priory Green who have welcomed us with warmth and grace and thrown themselves into everything we offer. We have loved getting to know them and are so pleased to be sharing their stories with you.

It's often said that you don't remember what people say as much as how they make you feel. We believe that soup is the ultimate way to make people feel good: an expression of love and care through food that can't be beaten. This book has been created to bring that love and care from our community to yours. We hope you enjoy it.

Karen Mattison and Robinne Collie, Co-Founders

*Where it all began...*

# MARTHA AHMET

Martha Ahmet knows Islington. She knows its streets. She knows its people. She grew up off the Holloway Road and left school at a young age. She was 21 when she had her first child, and by 29 she was a mother of four – and fairly desperate.

"The kids were young, my husband wasn't working at the time, and our electricity was about to get cut off," she says. So when asked if she could use a keyboard to work as a call-handler at the London Radio Taxis Group in Finsbury Park, she said yes. "I was petrified, and I was pretty sure it was like a typewriter," she said. "I thought: how hard can it be? I just really needed that job."

And she got the job despite never having used a keyboard in her life. She ended up working for that firm for 20 years, going on to become a supervisor and then a senior supervisor before being tasked with creating a training department and became the training manager.

It was there she discovered that she had a talent for bringing out the best in people and for making them believe in themselves. "I wanted to help people learn new skills and progress within the company, because I knew how mundane the job could be," she said. "I wanted them to feel more confident."

Now, around 40 years after starting that first job, Martha is using that talent every day as Cook for Good's Community Manager. But she is much more than that. She is the soul of the operation – an embodiment of its spirit and purpose.

"What makes me feel so connected to this place is that I know it only too well, having lived around here for many years," she says. "I know what it is not to have enough to give your children what they need. It's painful. When you hit rock bottom like that, you just feel so small, you just feel so down, everybody's so much better than you. I know how hard it is to grow from that."

Every member or volunteer you speak to about Cook for Good talks about Martha. She's considered an angel or a benign bully – someone who helps take others to places they thought they could never get to, places they thought weren't for people like them. "These are all people, and everybody, everybody, has got something special to offer," she says. "Everybody can come out of wherever they are. If you have the desire to, you can do it … you just sometimes need somebody to make you realise that you want to."

When Cook for Good started and Martha heard about the concept of the Pantry, she wanted the customers using it to feel like they were shopping at Waitrose. On Thursdays, they can browse the fresh fruit and veg on offer, all displayed in rustic wooden crates. Top quality tinned goods are presented with care, and after doing their shopping, customers can sit and have a cup of tea or coffee, their purchases at their feet.

"There are three things people get here," she explains. "One is dignity, the second is choice, and the third is trust. No one feels looked down on when they come in here. They are just doing their weekly shop."

And if they are going through a bad patch in their lives, there is always someone to listen. "They know that we will do anything that we can," she says. "But they will also be made to feel that they are needed too."

Martha, who started part-time, has been promoted, works full-time, and says she can't imagine ever doing anything else. "I always say the day I got this job is the day I retired, because if you find your passion, you'll never need to work another day in your life," she says. "I learn so much from this community – as much as they learn from us. But I love that when somebody walks in here with a sad face, we are able to help them walk out with a smile. That just gives me so much satisfaction."

She loves the sense of companionship the older men get from the Men's Grub Club and the happy hubbub of the Thursday Pantry, but the cooking classes for local children are perhaps her favourite. "It makes me really happy when I go over to the kitchen and see those kids cooking with their parents. I hear them come into the Pantry and see them learning how to deal with different problems together," she says. "I'm so proud of the fact that we have opened the doors to a better future for the children here."

Asked why she thinks this place works, she lights up. "Open your door, sit around a table, share your bread, talk," she says. "It's simple, but it's magical."

*Interview by Alexandra Topping*

# A FEW TIPS
# AND TRICKS

Whipping up soup on a weekly basis has given us a whole new insight on what works best to make the most fabulous bowls full of nourishment. Here are some of our top tips and tricks to help you achieve soup success.

## POTS AND PANS

You can make soup in most cooking vessels but it's helpful to use a large saucepan or a shallow casserole pan – they have lower sides than a deep stock pot which helps you get a bit of caramelised colour on your base vegetables before adding your stock. If you only have a frying pan and a stock pot, cook your vegetable base in a frying pan then add everything to a stock pot for the slow simmer stage.

## OIL AND BUTTER

Some of our soups are luxuriously smooth and creamy. A bit of healthy fat helps achieve this but if you're on a lower fat diet you can reduce the oil or butter – just add a little water, if needed, when sautéing the vegetables to prevent sticking. If you're vegan or dairy-free, you can swap butter for oil. And do feel free to swap out recommended oils – we've gone for our preferences for each soup but do take the liberty to use what you have and what you love.

## GET YOUR STOCK SIMMERING

To help your soup cook faster and to make it super-smooth and creamy, if blending, warm your stock in a saucepan as your other ingredients are cooking.

## BLENDING YOUR SOUP

We love a smooth and velvety blended soup. A stick blender is one of the easiest bits of kit to use; it's affordable, easy to clean and you can stick it straight into your pot to fully or part blend your soup. That said, large jug blenders make for extra smooth soups, but let your ingredients cool a little before adding, as the heat pressure can cause a volcanic-like eruption – messy and potentially dangerous. Food processors are also good but sometimes they require a longer blend to get your soup super smooth.

# THE MAGIC OF HOMEMADE STOCK

**Prep time:**
10 minutes

**Cooking time:**
12 minutes for vegetable stock,
2 hours for chicken or beef stock

**Makes 1 litre**

Stocks are the backbone of all good soups, like liquid gold that help all your main ingredients shine. Swap the stock out for water and you'll notice the difference. Having a supply of good stock cubes to hand means you can whip up a soup with speed. But a home-made stock adds a layer of good-ness and is free of sugar and yeast, while also allowing you to control the salt level more. This recipe is one of the easiest and fastest you'll find.

## METHOD

Peel and finely chop your carrots and onions. Finely chop your celery or fennel. Set a large saucepan or shallow casserole pan over medium heat. Add the olive oil and the veg. Lower the heat. Season with salt and pepper. Cook for 2 minutes, or until the veg have started to soften. Pour in the water. Bring to the boil. Turn off the heat. Stand for 10 mins. Strain through a fine mesh sieve. Squeeze out as much liquid as you can.

If you're not using it immediately, cool your stock fully. Decant into a lidded container: big yogurt pots or ice cube trays are great. Store in the fridge for up to a week or freeze for up to a year. Defrost instantly in a saucepan over a medium heat, or overnight in the fridge.

**STOCK BOOSTERS**     In addition to the carrot, onion and celery or fennel base, you can add any of the following: leafy green carrot tops, sweetcorn husks, silks and cobs, parsnips, squash or pumpkin trimmings, celeriac, summer bean or asparagus trimmings. A few herbs or spices are nice, too: parsley, bay leaves, tarragon, fennel seeds, saffron, cinnamon stick, cumin seeds, coriander seeds, cloves, star anise, fresh ginger, lemon grass, turmeric, chilli.

**CHICKEN OR BEEF STOCK**     For a bone-based stock, you'll want to cook everything much slower and longer to help draw the collagen from the bones (which is great for gut health). Cut the veg into 4cm chunks. Add to the pan with the oil to lightly colour. Add raw or leftover roasted meat bones and cook a little to warm through, then add enough water to fully cover. Lower heat and simmer for 1 ½ hours. Take off the heat. Cool for 30 minutes, then strain and use immediately or store as above.

## INGREDIENTS

**4** carrots

**2** onions

**2** celery sticks
or **1** fennel bulb

**2** garlic cloves

**1 tbsp** olive oil

**1.25 litre** water

Salt and pepper

# A WORLD OF CHICKEN SOUP

Chicken soup has been known for centuries as a comfort food that has almost magical healing powers. And despite the developments in modern medicine, it is still used all over the world to offer comfort and care to friends and family who are feeling unwell or in need of some extra love. Every culture has its own chicken soup, and we've tried many different versions over the last few years. These recipes are some of our community's favourites.

**Prep time:**

15 minutes

**Cooking time:**

3½ hours minimum

**Serves 4–6**

# TRADITIONAL JEWISH CHICKEN SOUP

Our founders come from a long line of chicken soup makers and are firm believers in the health benefits it brings. It's known informally as Jewish penicillin, and during lockdown, Karen made doorstep deliveries to friends and neighbours who had caught Covid. There's no definitive version of this soup as the recipe tends to be passed down through the generations; every family thinks theirs is the best, but this is how we like it. Best served at least 24 hours after cooking, this soup just gets better and better.

## INGREDIENTS

**1** whole chicken or

**1** chicken carcass + pack of wings

**2** onions

**2** celery sticks

**2** leeks

**3–4** large carrots

**1** small swede

**4** stock cubes (**2** beef, **2** chicken)

**2 litres** hot water

Salt and pepper

## METHOD

Place the chicken or carcass and wings into a large saucepan. Fill the pan with enough water to cover the chicken. Bring to the boil and skim off any scum that rises to the top of the pan.

Meanwhile, halve the onions. Keep the skins on for colour and extra flavour. Chop the celery and leeks into large chunks. Peel and cut the carrots into large chunks. Peel and cut the swede into smaller chunks. Add all the vegetables to the pan with the chicken, crumble in the stock cubes and add the 2 litres of hot water (or dissolve the cubes in the hot water first then add). Top up with more stock or water to ensure all the ingredients are submerged. Cover with a lid, bring back to the boil, then turn down to a very low simmer and cook covered for a minimum of 3 hours (keep on a low simmer to make sure it doesn't boil away). Alternatively, you can put the soup in the oven at 150°C/ Gas mark 2 and cook for 6–7 hours to get an even deeper flavour.

When done, remove from the heat and add salt and pepper to taste. Sieve the soup into another container (to remove the chicken and vegetables and to assist cooling).

You can keep the soup as a clear broth or you may prefer to add some of the chicken back in (off the bone and shredded) and any vegetables you like e.g., the cooked carrots, sliced.

When cool enough, refrigerate or freeze in suitable containers or freezer bags. Once chilled, there is often a layer of fat at the top which you can simply scrape away before reheating until piping hot.

**"** We love meeting up and getting together. The soup reaches deep into places that other things just can't reach. **"**

*Pantry member*

## EMERGENCY CHICKEN NOODLE SOUP

**Prep time:**
15 minutes

**Cooking time:**
15–20 minutes

**Serves 4–6**

We all have those days when we're in a rush and just need a quick, satisfying meal that everyone will like. This is the recipe we reach for: a simple soup that's easy to throw together and balances protein, veg, and carbs in one bowl. If you want to ramen it up, just add some soy, sliced ginger, and coriander stalks or a stick of bashed up lemongrass and serve with a scattering of chopped coriander leaves.

### INGREDIENTS

**1** onion

**1** garlic clove

**2** carrots

**1** celery stick

**350g** cooked chicken (thigh meat is our favourite)

**1 tbsp** butter

**1 tbsp** vegetable oil

**1** bay leaf

**1.75 litres** chicken stock

**250g** medium egg noodles

Salt and pepper

### METHOD

Peel and finely chop the onion and garlic. Peel and cut the carrots into 1cm dice. Cut the celery into 1cm dice. Slice the cooked chicken into 2cm pieces.

Place a large saucepan or shallow casserole pan on a medium heat and add the butter and oil. Add the onion, carrot, and celery and sauté for 5 minutes or until starting to soften. Stir in the garlic and bay leaf. Season with salt and pepper. Cook for a further minute.

Add the stock to the pan. Bring to the boil and then stir in the chicken. Bring back to the boil and simmer for a further 2 minutes. Add the noodles to the pan and cook until they are al dente, around 3 minutes.

Remove the bay leaf and season to taste.

**Prep time:**
10 minutes

**Cooking time:**
30 minutes

Serves 4-6

# CHINESE-STYLE CHICKEN AND SWEETCORN SOUP

We served this as a starter at a community meal to celebrate Chinese New Year and it went down a treat with our guests; they almost didn't have enough space for their homemade fortune cookies. Our version of the classic Chinese favourite, it's packed full of lean protein and hearty flavours. It's a great way of using up leftover cooked chicken too – just skip the first stage of the recipe.

## INGREDIENTS

**2** skinless chicken breast fillets

**1.5 litres** chicken stock

**1 tbsp** vegetable oil

**2** garlic cloves

A small **thumb** of ginger (approx. **5 cm**)

**2** eggs

**300 g** sweetcorn kernels (frozen or drained tinned)

**1 tbsp** light soy sauce

**3 tbsp** cornflour

**2** spring onions

**1 tbsp** sesame oil

## METHOD

Place the chicken breasts in a large saucepan and cover with stock. Bring to the boil, then lower the heat, cover, and simmer for 10–15 minutes or until the chicken is cooked through.

Meanwhile, peel and finely chop the garlic. Peel and finely grate the ginger. Beat the eggs with a fork or whisk until the yolk and whites are well combined.

Once cooked through, remove the chicken breasts from the stock, allow to cool enough to handle, then finely shred using a fork. Keep the remaining stock.

Set a large saucepan or shallow casserole pan on a medium heat. Once hot, add the oil, garlic, and ginger, frying it until fragrant and just golden. Add the sweetcorn and soy sauce and continue to fry for a further 3 minutes, stirring regularly. Pour in the stock and bring to the boil.

Mix the cornflour with enough water (3–4 tbsp) to make a paste in a small bowl. Slowly add the cornflour mixture in a thin drizzle to the soup while stirring – the soup should start to thicken. Stir in the shredded chicken. Slowly drizzle the whisked eggs into the soup and use a spoon, moving it back and forth across the top of the soup, to slowly break up the egg as it cooks, and form it into "strings."

Take the soup off the heat. Thinly slice the spring onions. Finish off the soup by stirring in the spring onions. Drizzle a little sesame oil over the top. Dash in a little more soya sauce to taste.

**TOP IT OFF**    Lovely with chilli flakes and fresh coriander leaves.

**Prep time:**
25 minutes

**Cooking time:**
25 minutes

**Serves 4–6**

# THAI CHICKEN NOODLE SOUP

When team member Cathy's daughter asked for some noodle soup recipes to take back to university, there was only one answer: this fabulous, hearty Thai version. The aromatic curry paste combined with the creamy sweetness of the coconut milk creates a rich, warming soup that is as tasty as it is filling. It's proved a real hit with a houseful of students up in Leeds.

## INGREDIENTS

**1** onion

**3** garlic cloves

**3** carrots

**1** red pepper

**3** large skinless, boneless, chicken breasts

**150g** rice noodles

½ lime

**2 tbsp** olive oil

**4 tbsp** red curry paste

**1 litre** chicken stock

**500ml** coconut milk

½ **tsp** ground black pepper

**20g** fresh coriander

¾ **tsp** chilli flakes

Salt and pepper

## METHOD

Peel and finely chop the onion and garlic. Peel and cut the carrots into 1cm dice. Halve the red pepper, remove the stem and seeds, and cut into 1cm dice. Cut the chicken breasts into 1cm dice. Break up the rice noodles. Juice the lime.

Set a large saucepan or shallow casserole pan on a medium heat. Add the oil, followed by the onion, carrot, and red pepper and sauté for 3–4 minutes, stirring constantly. Add the chicken and mix well. Add the garlic and curry paste. Cook until the chicken is just cooked, around 3–4 minutes. Mix in the stock and coconut milk. Season with a little salt and pepper. Bring the soup to the boil and let it cook for a further 5 minutes.

Finely chop the coriander and set aside for garnish. Add the broken noodles to the soup and bring back to the boil. Reduce heat to low and simmer for around 3 minutes. Test for the balance of flavours and add chilli flakes and lime juice to taste. Season with salt and pepper as needed.

Serve the soup warm. Finish with the chopped coriander.

**Prep time:**
25 minutes

**Cooking time:**
50 minutes

**Serves 4–6**

## INGREDIENTS

**500g** chicken mince

**85g** breadcrumbs

**1** egg

**30g** flat-leaf parsley

A pinch of garlic salt (optional)

**2 tbsp** vegetable oil

**1** onion

**2** garlic cloves

**2** carrots

**1.2 litres** chicken stock

**1** bay leaf

**15g** dill

**140g** orzo

Salt and pepper

## NO STRESS BREAD
Lovely with our rosemary and garlic focaccia.

# OUR ITALIAN WEDDING SOUP

A modern twist on the traditional Italian wedding soup, which you don't have to be getting married to enjoy. We first made this for our Pantry members on a cold February day, and they absolutely loved it. Juicy meatballs combined with filling orzo pasta and flavoured with aromatic dill and parsley… it's a bowl full of comfort and joy. If you're making this soup ahead of time, leave the orzo out, then pop it in for 10 minutes while you're warming it up to serve.

## METHOD

Preheat oven to 180°C/Gas mark 4.

Put the chicken mince, breadcrumbs, and egg in a large bowl. Finely chop the parsley, put half in the bowl with the chicken, and reserve the rest for later. Add a pinch of garlic salt, salt, and black pepper to the chicken and combine everything well. Shape small meatballs from the mix, roughly 1 heaped tablespoon per meatball, and place them on a baking tray lined with non-stick baking paper. The mix should yield between 25 and 30 meatballs. Bake on the top shelf of the oven for 15 minutes until golden.

Peel and finely chop the onion and garlic. Peel and cut the carrots into 1cm dice.

Place a large saucepan or shallow casserole pan over a medium heat. Once warm, add the oil and the chopped onion and carrot. Sauté for 10–15 minutes until they begin to caramelise, stirring often. When it's nicely golden, add the garlic, lower the heat to medium, and sauté for a minute longer or until fragrant. Finely chop the dill and set aside.

Once the meatballs are out of the oven, add them to the pan with the softened veg and pour in the stock. Season with salt and pepper. Add three quarters of the chopped dill, the bay leaf, and half of the remaining parsley. Reserve the rest of the chopped herbs for garnish.

Cover the pan with a lid and cook for 10 minutes. Stir in the orzo and cook for another 10–12 minutes until tender. Serve garnished with the reserved parsley and chopped dill.

# NICHOLAS SINCLAIR

Nicholas wasn't really thinking about himself when he came to the Pantry for the first time. He'd been caring for his 83-year-old mum for a while and was worried about her becoming isolated. The doctor had told him that being sociable could really help, so he brought her along.

"During Covid we were just stuck at home – I suppose everyone was – and it was like we were going crazy," he says over a cup of tea in the Pantry. "But here you meet people all the time. It's brought a lot of connections and friends into our lives. Mum suffers from depression and just being out here in the community among people makes the world of difference. She's made really good friends, and she looks forward to coming – she's much healthier, much happier."

Nicholas, now 60, brought his mum to a cooking demo, hoping she might get a little more interested in cooking. And while the class didn't motivate her to get creative in the kitchen, it did have a profound impact on him. "I was at the very first demo before they opened up the kitchen," he recalls. "It's remarkable what they've done here and how far they've come."

He started to attend more demos, and when the opportunity arose for him to get more involved, he leapt at the chance. "I've found that I quite enjoy cooking," he says. "So I cook a lot at home and I've learned a lot from just being here, a lot of new skills. I've learned how to chop an onion properly for a start!"

As someone who was at risk of developing diabetes, Nicholas was eligible to join a bespoke course, Cook for Health. This has changed how he thinks about food and taught him how to cook healthier meals. "I love learning in that kind of environment; it's a really great atmosphere," he says.

He still expresses incredulity when he describes how the participants on the course were able to speak to three doctors who were giving advice – at no cost. "They planned the classes, and we learned about plant-based cooking and how to make healthier choices. They were really helpful," he states. "Three GPs in a class! You can't even get to see one GP at the doctor's surgery so that was really brilliant."

He's also participated and made new friends in the Men's Grub Club. "I look forward to any cooking opportunities. They have cooking demos here as well, so I put my name down and come along and see professional chefs. I've picked up some really good tips." Now he wants to learn how to bake and to start making his own stock for soups. "When you start looking at the ingredients on food packaging, you just think 'what is all this stuff?' So now I want to make meals where you know what has gone into them."

Gaining cooking skills is only part of what is on offer though, says Nicholas. He was also encouraged to apply for a cooker replacement, as his mum's old one took hours to cook a meal.

"Cook for Good has all sorts of different people coming in. There are people to talk to you about the type of help you can get or to give you advice about saving money on your energy bills. It's like they are trying to cover a whole range of things," he says. "And the staff here are like angels; they're just so amazing and so caring."

While his mum sits and chats with her friends at the Pantry, he does her shopping and then also has a sit down and a coffee. "It's helped me as well," he shares. "I just really connected with everyone. Sometimes my mum doesn't come along, and I'll come on my own. I'm always talking about Cook for Good to people; I tell everyone about it because they are just amazing here."

Nicholas laughs that his sister is always complaining that there isn't a similar organisation where she lives. He recently invited her to a community meal, a Cook for Good event where new and old guests come together to share food prepared by a group of company employees who have been cooking in the kitchen as part of a teambuilding day.

"She absolutely loved it," he reports. "There are so many lonely people in this country, but here all of us join together and do something that we all enjoy. It brings us all together."

*Interview by Alexandra Topping*

**Prep time:**
15 minutes, plus minimum
30 minutes soaking

**Cooking time:**
25 minutes

**Serves 4–6**

# GREEK AVGOLEMONO SOUP

This modern take on the classic Greek soup is the perfect remedy for anyone feeling feverish and achy and a great preventative elixir and immune booster as well. Adding some healthy seasonal greens towards the end will provide a vitamin hit as well as a flavour boost, and the fresh lemon isn't just there to make it taste extra special; it also helps draw out the iron from the green veg.

## INGREDIENTS

**200g** white basmati rice

**2 tbsp** olive oil

**2.5 litres** chicken stock

**200g** cooked chicken
(leftover from a roasted
chicken or a poached breast)

**4** garlic cloves

**4** lemons

**3** eggs

Salt and pepper

### SEASONAL EXTRAS

**150g** seasonal greens

**1** leek or **8** spring onions

**1 tbsp** fresh thyme or
chopped parsley to finish

## METHOD

Soak the rice in clean cold water for at least 30 minutes or ideally overnight. Shred the cooked chicken with a fork. Peel and finely chop the garlic. Zest two of the lemons and juice enough to yield 200ml.

Drain and rinse the rice. Set a large saucepan or shallow casserole pan on a medium heat. Add the rice and olive oil to the pan with a pinch of sea salt and toast for a couple of minutes, stirring as you do. Pour in the stock. Add the shredded chicken, pop a lid on, and simmer for 12–15 minutes or until the rice is fully tender. Once the rice is cooked, add the chopped garlic and grated lemon zest.

Put the lemon juice in a medium bowl, crack in the eggs, and whisk to mix through. Spoon a few ladles of the warm stock into the lemon and egg mixture to gently warm it, whisking all the time, then slowly add the lemon and egg mixture into the soup, stirring constantly.

Finely shred the seasonal greens if using. Trim and finely slice the leek or spring onions. Add the leeks or spring onions and seasonal greens and simmer for about 5 minutes until just softened.

Taste and adjust seasoning, adding more lemon too if you think it needs it. If the soup thickens too much, you can add some more stock. Spoon into bowls and finish with fresh herbs.

# CHICKEN AND WHITE BEAN SOUP WITH WALNUT PESTO

A terrific soup that is bursting with flavours. It's delicious as it is, but it's worth including the homemade pesto – it only takes a few minutes to make from scratch and adds a freshness that takes this soup to a whole new level. We love cannellini beans best, but any white beans (such as pillowy butter beans) will work so feel free to substitute with your favourite.

## INGREDIENTS

**2 tbsp** olive oil

**2** chicken breasts (skin on)

**1** large onion

**3** garlic cloves

**2** carrots

**2** celery sticks

**3** sprigs of thyme

**1** bay leaf

**1 litre** chicken stock

**2 × 400g** tins white beans

**10g** parsley

**1** lemon

Salt and pepper

### WALNUT PESTO

**40g** Parmesan or Pecorino cheese

**1–2** garlic cloves

**60g** baby spinach

Juice of ½ lemon – you can use lemon from the soup

**½ tsp** salt (to taste)

**150ml** olive oil

**60g** walnuts

## METHOD

Peel and finely chop the onion and garlic. Peel and cut the carrots into 2cm dice. Cut the celery into 2cm dice. Strip the thyme leaves from the stalks and discard the stalks.

Set a large saucepan or shallow casserole pan over a medium heat. Once hot, add the olive oil. Place the chicken breasts in the pan skin side down. Cook until golden brown. Then turn the breasts over to cook the other side until golden. Remove the chicken and set aside for later.

Place the pan you used for the chicken, with the oil and pan juices still inside, over a low heat. Add the onion, thyme, bay leaf, and a good pinch of salt. Cook until translucent, stirring regularly, for about 10–15 minutes. Drain the tins of beans, rinse, and set aside.

Add the garlic, carrot, and celery to the pan and fry for a couple of minutes. Add the stock. Bring to a gentle simmer. Then add the chicken and poach for 15 minutes or until tender. Remove the chicken breasts from the soup. Strip off the skin and shred the meat with a fork.

Add the shredded chicken back to the pan together with the drained beans. Season with salt and pepper to taste. Simmer gently for 8–10 minutes.

Finely chop the parsley. Grate the zest of the lemon into the pan and add the juice of half the lemon.

For the pesto, finely grate the cheese. Peel one of the garlic cloves. Add both to a blender with the spinach, juice of half a lemon, and a pinch of salt. Then add the olive oil and blend. Finally, add the walnuts and pulse until roughly chopped to give you a coarse texture. Taste, add more garlic if needed, and season to taste.

Once the soup is ready, add the chopped parsley and serve in bowls with a spoonful of pesto.

**PESTO TIP**     Store the pesto with a drizzle of oil over the top. It will keep in the fridge for up to 3 days or in the freezer for up to 6 months.

**Prep time:**
10 minutes

**Cooking time:**
50 minutes

**Serves 4–6**

# MEXICAN CHICKEN AND BLACK BEAN SOUP

This soup turns any meal into a fiesta and brings a touch of spice and a whole load of warmth to our Pantry. We love to serve it on a chilly winter's day, and it's become a real favourite with our members; it's probably one of the soups they request the most. It's well worth adding the sprinkling of coriander just before you serve for an extra fresh aroma and taste.

## INGREDIENTS

**1 litre** vegetable or chicken stock

**1** large chicken breast

**2 tbsp** olive oil

**1** onion

**2** garlic cloves

**1** large red pepper

**1 tsp** ground cumin

**1 tsp** ground coriander

**½ tsp** smoked paprika

**½ tsp** mild chilli powder

**2 × 400g** tins chopped tomatoes

**1 × 400g** tin black beans
(can use pinto or any beans)

**100g** sweetcorn kernels
(frozen or tinned)

Salt and pepper

## METHOD

Pour your stock into a large saucepan and set over a medium heat. Once the stock is warm and steamy, add the chicken breast and cook for 10–15 minutes or until no longer pink in the middle. Remove the chicken from the stock (keep the stock to use as the base for the soup). Allow the poached chicken breast to cool a little and then shred it finely using a fork.

Peel and finely chop the onion and garlic. Finely dice the red pepper. Set the saucepan you used for the chicken over a medium heat. Add the oil to the pan along with the onion, garlic, and a pinch of salt. Sweat slowly until tender, but don't let it pick up any colour. Add the red pepper and sauté for 3 minutes or until just tender. Fold in the cumin, coriander, paprika, and chilli powder and cook until aromatic. Add the stock and bring to the boil, then turn down, and simmer for 10 minutes. Add the tinned tomatoes and bring to the boil again, then turn down to simmer for another 15 minutes.

Drain the beans and sweetcorn (if tinned). Stir them into the soup along with the shredded chicken. Simmer for 10 minutes to warm through and marry the flavours. Taste and add salt and pepper as needed.

**TOP IT OFF**     We love it with fresh coriander and grated cheese. For an added boost, whip up our favourite salsa.

**NO STRESS BREAD**     Delicious with our cornbread.

# IJEOMA ANYANWU

Ijeoma Anyanwu was 30 when she arrived in the UK from Nigeria. She had a degree in industrial chemistry and thought finding a job and settling into her new married life would be easy.

"For months and months, I couldn't find anything," she says, adding that she would often get interviews but not be chosen for the job. "My husband, who was born in this country, said it might be because of the environment and the cultural differences and that I had to work on my communication skills."

But it wasn't just the difficulty in finding a job matching her skills that was a challenge for Ijeoma. The 34-year-old had come from a tight-knit community and was a member of a large family. In London she felt adrift, lonely, and homesick.

"At home it felt there was more of a sense of community, a kind of natural friendliness," she says. "I come from a place that is very family-orientated, and even if you are not part of the family by blood, it still feels like you belong."

She admits to having felt bored and unchallenged. "I didn't want to sit at home and relax; I always want to be doing something. So I cooked a lot, but my husband is only one man and couldn't eat all the food I made!"

The situation became harder still after she had her first child. She started working in retail, working nights while her husband worked during the day so that they could care for their child. After having a second baby, she had a sudden realisation about her future path.

"I thought 'this is not where I want to be, this is not what I want to do.' I wanted to do something I loved, not even what I studied at university," she says. "I had only just had our second baby when I told my husband, 'I think I need to go into catering. I need to get out, I feel I am trapped, and I need to be free.'"

Her husband was supportive and told her to start looking online for catering and culinary courses, but she soon saw that the cost was well out of their price range. But then fate intervened.

Ijeoma had been volunteering as a parent champion at The Parent House in Islington. Part of her role was to point other women who felt isolated or were in need towards the support they could get. A colleague at the charity, who knew about her quest for a new direction, shared a flyer with her about Cook for Good's Community Brigade programme.

"I immediately thought this is God in heaven listening to my plea," she laughs. "I had just been looking online for something like this, and now the opportunity comes. I called straight away to schedule an interview, because I was so worried there would be no spaces left on the course."

Community Manager Martha met the young mother, who brought her sleeping two-month-old along to the interview, and showed her the kitchen where she would be learning new skills. "I had never seen anything like it," Ijeoma recalls. "It was like a dream. I looked and I thought: this is the place I want to be!"

The impact of the course on her life was immediate. She loved cooking and she loved creating, but most of all she loved the sense of belonging.

"Everyone was so lovely to me, it was like I was back home again," she says. "I said to them on graduation day that it was the best thing I had done in my life. I have done lots of courses but Cook for Good was the best. It brought out the best in me, it built up my confidence, and it gave me so many new skills."

Now Ijeoma has qualifications in knife skills, food hygiene, and safety. She has done work experience: her first stints were in professional kitchens in the offices of Spotify and a City law firm. She has also worked on a soup lunch project with her Brigade colleagues, making big batches of soup and taking it into different companies to serve to employees.

"What I love so much about the soup lunches is seeing people smile and enjoy what I have made," she says. "I can see it gives them pleasure, and I love that."

Now Ijeoma is looking to do shifts with the catering company where she did her work experience and with Cook for Good, so she can work flexibly around the needs of her children. "This place has helped shape my life," she says. "I was a naive, shy little girl, but now I am bold. Where I am right now – that's where I want to be."

*Interview by Alexandra Topping*

# WEST AFRICAN PEANUT AND CHICKEN SOUP

Based on a centuries-old recipe, this soup was traditionally known as Groundnut Stew and has its origins in West Africa, where groundnuts have long been a staple food. Our version uses peanuts and peanut butter, which blend beautifully with the other ingredients to make a rich, flavourful soup. As the recipe suggests, it can be eaten on a bed of rice, which makes it more stew-like, but it's equally delicious on its own as a lighter meal.

## INGREDIENTS

**2** onions

**1** medium sweet potato

**150g** baby spinach

**200g** cooked chicken
(from leftover roast chicken
or poached chicken breast)

**60g** roasted peanuts
(salted or unsalted)

A small thumb of ginger
(approx. **5cm**)

**2 tbsp** vegetable oil

**85g** tomato puree

**1 tsp** cayenne pepper (use
less for milder soup)

**1.25 litres** vegetable stock

**260g** smooth (unsweetened)
peanut butter

**120g** white basmati rice

Salt and pepper

## METHOD

Peel and finely chop the onions. Peel and cut the sweet potato into 1cm dice. Wash and drain the spinach if needed and shred the cooked chicken with a fork. Chop the peanuts. Peel and finely grate the ginger.

Set a large saucepan or shallow casserole pan on a medium heat. Once hot, add the oil along with the onions and grated ginger and cook gently for 10 minutes until the onions are soft but not coloured. Add the tomato puree, mix well, and then add in the sweet potatoes. Season with a good pinch of salt and cayenne pepper.

Pour the stock into the pan and bring to the boil. Lower the heat and simmer for 10 minutes, by which time the sweet potatoes should be cooked. Meanwhile, cook the rice in a separate pan according to the pack instructions.

Once the sweet potatoes are tender, stir in the peanut butter thoroughly. Add the spinach and shredded chicken and stir well.

Serve the soup hot over white rice garnished with the chopped peanuts.

“ Since I started coming here, I have
felt such a warm community spirit.
I don't just come for the food – it is the
welcome and the community feeling. ”

*Pantry member*

# TWO WAYS WITH...

Our fresh Pantry produce is seasonal so it's not unusual for us to receive a big pile of one particular veg. We love finding new and inventive ways to use them up and run regular Two Ways With... cooking demos in our Community Kitchen, where we experiment with different recipes based on the same base food. These are tried and tested soups that turn an everyday ingredient into a couple of special meals.

# BUTTERNUT, SWEET POTATO, AND COCONUT SOUP

One of Pantry Manager Tom's favourite things is hearing members chatting about using our recipes to cook an ingredient they've never tried before. As he says, it's a great example of food bringing people together. We created this soup to encourage people to try using butternut squash. It's a tasty, warming bowl with creamy coconut, health-boosting ginger, and a bit of a kick. There's an ongoing debate among our members about whether soups should be smooth or chunky, but we all agree this one is best blended to a velvety texture.

## INGREDIENTS

**1kg** butternut squash

**300g** sweet potatoes

**1** onion

A small thumb of ginger (approx. **5cm**)

½ fresh red chilli

**1 tsp** chilli flakes (add only as much as you like)

**2–3 tbsp** butter (can replace with olive oil to keep soup vegan)

**1 × 400ml** tin coconut milk

**1 litre** vegetable stock

Salt and pepper

## METHOD

Wash and slice the butternut squash in half lengthways and remove the seeds. There's no need to peel it! Cut the butternut into 3cm dice. Peel the sweet potato and cut into 2cm dice. Peel and finely chop the onion. Peel and grate the ginger. Deseed and thinly slice the chilli.

Set a large saucepan or shallow casserole pan on a medium heat. Add 2 tablespoons of butter or olive oil, followed by all the prepared vegetables, ginger, and fresh chilli. For additional spice, add half a teaspoon of chilli flakes.

Gently sauté for at least 10 minutes – you're not wanting colour, just a slow cook until the veg is translucent, so keep the heat low and stir regularly. Add the coconut milk and stock and season with salt and pepper as needed. Bring to the boil, then turn down to a simmer and cook until the vegetables are soft, about 30 minutes.

When the vegetables are soft, blend until smooth. Finally, check the seasoning and adjust to taste with salt, pepper, and additional chilli flakes.

**TOP IT OFF**     Serve drizzled with a little olive oil, chilli flakes, and chopped coriander.

*See page 49 for soup image*

**Prep time:**
10 minutes

**Cooking time:**
45 minutes

**Serves 6**

# ROASTED BUTTERNUT SQUASH SOUP

This recipe is a game-changer for anyone who loves butternut squash soup but hates the faff of peeling it. Roasting isn't just easier; it also adds a richness and depth to the flavour. You can swap the squash for other root vegetables and use different spices to jazz things up further. Our resident chef, Simone, loves adding ras el hanout and harissa to give it a Moroccan vibe.

## INGREDIENTS

**1** large butternut squash

**1** large carrot

**2 tbsp** olive oil, for roasting

**1** onion

**2 tbsp** olive oil, for sautéing

**1** leek

**1.25 litres** vegetable stock

Salt and pepper

## METHOD

Preheat oven to 190°C/Gas mark 5. Wash, halve, and deseed the butternut squash. There's no need to peel it! Cut into 3cm chunks. Wash and roughly chop the carrot. Put the butternut squash and carrot cubes in a large bowl and mix well with the 3 tablespoons of olive oil for roasting. Season with plenty of salt and pepper. Line a baking tray with non-stick baking paper. Arrange the butternut squash and carrot on the baking tray in an even single layer. Cook in the oven until tender, around 20 minutes.

Peel and dice the onion. Set a large saucepan or shallow casserole pan over a medium heat. Add the remaining olive oil along with the diced onion. Gently cook – you're not wanting colour but just a slow cook so keep the heat low and stir regularly.

Wash the leek and thinly slice. Add to the pan to sauté along with the onion. Once tender, add the roasted butternut squash and carrot. Pour in the stock and mix well. Bring the pan to the boil, then turn down to a simmer and cook until the vegetables are soft, approximately 25 minutes.

When the vegetables are soft, blend the soup until smooth. Season with salt and pepper to taste. Serve piping hot.

**TOP IT OFF**     We love this soup with garlic and herb croutons. It's also wonderful with a finishing touch of herb oil or herb-infused cream and chilli flakes.

**NO STRESS BREAD**     A truly delightful partner for this comforting soup is our cheese, onion, and garlic soda bread.

TOP: Butternut, sweet potato, and coconut soup

BOTTOM: Roasted butternut squash soup

**Prep time:**
15 minutes

**Cooking time:**
50 minutes

**Serves 4–6**

# MARTHA'S FAVOURITE CAULIFLOWER CHEESE SOUP

There are few things better than a homemade cauliflower cheese, but we think this might just beat it. Community Manager Martha is inevitably at the front of the queue when it's served; she just loves its warmth and creaminess and always adds more cheese than the recipe says. We made it at our very first Pantry soup demo, and it was a massive hit. Our members wolfed it down, and we even had people asking for the recipe on social media. We hope you enjoy it, too.

## INGREDIENTS

**1** onion

**2** garlic cloves (optional)

**¼** leek

**1** large cauliflower

**150g** mature cheddar cheese

**3 tbsp** butter

**2 tbsp** olive oil

**1–1.5 litres** vegetable stock

**1 tsp** Dijon mustard

**50ml** double cream (optional)

Salt and pepper

*See page 52 for soup image*

## METHOD

Peel and finely chop the onion and garlic. Remove outer leaves from the leek, split in half lengthways, and wash under running water. Then cut into long strips lengthways and slice across.

Remove all the outer leaves from the cauliflower and trim the stem (you don't need the leaves for the soup, but they are delicious steamed or roasted with garlic and oil as a veg side).

Chop the cauliflower florets and tender inner core into small, even-sized pieces. Coarsely grate the cheese and set aside.

Set a large saucepan or shallow casserole pan on a medium heat. Add the butter and the olive oil. Add the onion, garlic, leek, and a pinch of salt. Sauté until soft (not brown but nicely soft). Add the chopped cauliflower, mix it through, and cook for 1–2 minutes. Pour in 1 litre of stock and season with some salt and pepper.

Cook for 30 minutes until the vegetables are soft, topping up with more stock if needed to fully cover all the veg. Take off the heat and blend until smooth.

Add the grated cheese and mustard and blend again. You can also add some cream to make it richer. Check the seasoning and add salt and pepper to taste. Add more Dijon mustard and/or cheese if you wish.

**TOP IT OFF**   Serve with a little cheese on top, croutons, and chopped parsley.

TOP: Martha's favourite
cauliflower cheese soup

BOTTOM: Cauliflower
and coconut soup

Prep time:
10 minutes

Cooking time:
40 minutes, plus
15 minutes for garnish

Serves 4–6

# CAULIFLOWER AND COCONUT SOUP

Cauliflower is a real staple of our surplus food deliveries, and our community are always keen to hear new ways to use it. It felt like the ideal place to start when we were looking to expand our vegan repertoire. And here's the result: a nourishing, silky smooth, and rich soup packed with flavour and warmth which has now become a firm favourite with vegans and non-vegans alike.

## INGREDIENTS

**1** onion

**1** garlic clove

**750g** cauliflower

**100g** butter or coconut oil

**500ml** vegetable stock

**1 × 400g** tin coconut milk

**150g** double cream or coconut cream

Salt and pepper

### GARNISH

**50g** butter or coconut oil

**125g** cauliflower (florets only)

**1 tsp** cumin seeds

**1 tsp** nigella seeds

**50g** flaked or desiccated coconut

## METHOD

Peel and finely chop the onion and garlic. Remove all the outer leaves from the cauliflower (you don't need the leaves for the soup, but they are delicious steamed or roasted with garlic and oil). Cut the florets and stalk into 3–4cm pieces.

Set a large saucepan or shallow casserole pan on a medium heat. Add 75g of butter, followed by the onion and garlic, and sauté for around 8 minutes until soft but not coloured. Next, add the cauliflower pieces, vegetable stock, and coconut milk. Stir and bring to the boil and then simmer until the cauliflower is tender, around 20 minutes.

Take the soup off the heat and add the remaining butter or coconut oil and the cream. Stir well and then blend until really smooth. Taste and season with salt and pepper as needed.

To make the garnish, chop the remaining cauliflower into small 1–2cm pieces. Place 50g of butter into a frying pan on a high heat. When frothy, add the cauliflower pieces, cumin seeds, nigella seeds, and coconut. Cook until golden brown and aromatic.

To serve, heat the soup until piping hot. Decant into bowls and sprinkle with the cauliflower, coconut, and seeds and drizzle over any remaining butter from the pan.

**Prep time:**
10 minutes

**Cooking time:**
1 hour 15 minutes

**Serves 4–6**

## INGREDIENTS

**2kg** fresh plum tomatoes

**4 tbsp** olive oil

**8** garlic cloves

**3** red onions

**2 tsp** sugar

**750ml** vegetable stock

**30g** fresh basil leaves

Salt and pepper

### GARNISH

Fromage frais

# GORDON BROWN'S REAL TOMATO SOUP

Former Prime Minister Gordon is a fantastic ally who shares our determination to help change lives for the better and has championed our work in public and private. While he doesn't claim to be much of a cook, this soup is one of his specialties and is a recipe he returns to again and again. He has loved tomatoes from childhood, and still loves them today – with breakfast, in a curry... all kinds of ways. This soup is healthy, hearty, and in a totally different league to its tinned equivalent.

## METHOD

Preheat the oven to 190°C/Gas mark 5. Line a baking sheet with non-stick baking paper. Halve the tomatoes. Peel the garlic cloves. Peel the onions and slice into thin half-moons.

Place the tomatoes and garlic in the roasting tin and drizzle with 3 tablespoons of the olive oil. Season generously with salt and pepper. Roast in the oven for 40 minutes.

While the tomatoes are roasting, make the caramelised onions. Set a frying pan over a medium heat. Once hot, add the remaining tablespoon of oil. Add the onion and stir to coat with oil. Cook for around 20 minutes, stirring occasionally, until the onions turn golden and are caramelised. Add the sugar, mix well, and remove from the heat.

Strip the basil leaves from the stalks. Reserve a handful of smaller basil leaves to garnish the soup. Remove the tomatoes from the oven and blend with the basil leaves and caramelised onions until smooth.

Pour the blended tomatoes into a saucepan. Set over a medium heat and whisk in the stock. Bring to the boil, then lower the heat, and simmer for 10 minutes. Ladle into bowls and garnish with fromage frais and the reserved basil leaves.

**NO STRESS BREAD**   This soup goes down a treat when paired with our challah rolls or our Portuguese water bread (pictured).

# THE PANTRY'S ORIGINAL TOMATO AND RED LENTIL SOUP

Here's where it all started, with this simplest of recipes, which Karen brought along to the Pantry for her lunch one cold winter's day. Volunteer Mary asked what was in her flask, Karen offered her a taste... and it all took off from there. Within a week, our staff were bringing in enough to share with the volunteers; within a month, we were serving members two soups every Thursday. Two years later, here we are, with a book full of recipes and a shared love of soup.

## INGREDIENTS

**1** onion

**2** garlic cloves

**2 tsp** coriander seeds

**2 tsp** cumin seeds

**2 tbsp** olive oil or butter

**250g** red lentils

**2 × 400g** tins chopped tomatoes

**1 litre** vegetable stock

Salt and pepper

## METHOD

Peel and finely chop the onion and garlic. Crush the coriander and cumin seeds in a pestle and mortar.

Set a large saucepan or shallow casserole pan on a medium heat. Add the olive oil or butter along with the diced onion and garlic. Add a pinch of salt, lower the heat, and gently cook until soft but not coloured.

Add the cumin and coriander and toast for a minute or until fragrant. Stir in the lentils and stock. Bring to the boil, then lower the heat, and simmer for 15 minutes.

Stir in the tomatoes and a pinch of salt and pepper. Bring back up to boil, then lower the heat, and simmer for another 15 minutes, or until the lentils are tender. At this point, the soup is ready. You can serve as it is or, for a smoother consistency, blend or partially blend it.

# JAMES COPE

James had been through a traumatic few years before he started coming to Cook for Good. The 57-year-old had worked for many years as a support worker for people with mental health difficulties; it wasn't always an easy job, but he loved it.

But then he was seriously assaulted by a client, and the repercussions were severe. He suffered from anxiety, depression, and PTSD and had to take more than a year off. He eventually went back to work, but a second assault resulted in him being put on medication which meant he could no longer drive and wasn't well enough to carry on working.

"For the past three years, I kind of isolated myself," he says. "Work was important to me. I used to have a lot of banter in my life, but when I was away from work, I didn't have that anymore and that's when my loneliness started. I was deteriorating."

He admits that he's always found it difficult to reach out for help. "I felt lonely, but I didn't know who to turn to," he says. "I'm one of those people who finds it very difficult to ask for help and support. I just try and work things out myself and do it my own way – sometimes that can be a barrier."

One day, at a local day centre, he saw an advert for the Men's Grub Club – cooking courses for older men run by Cook for Good. He thought it might be an opportunity to improve some rusty cooking skills, and the fact that it was aimed at older men also caught his eye. He decided to sign up.

He admits that he was nervous the first time he walked through the door. "You don't know what you're walking into; you don't know if you'll like it or if you'll get on with people," he says. "But all those worries faded as soon as I put my pinny on along with 20 other men and went down to the kitchen and just started cooking. My mind was completely on learning how to cook."

He puts much of that ease down to the teaching staff. "They are so full of smiles and radiant. It feels like they really enjoy what they do."

He confesses that before starting the course his diet consisted of pies, chips, and other food that was unlikely to promote a return to good health. But he's learnt a huge amount about how to make homemade dishes that are both delicious and good for you. "It gives me such pleasure cooking from scratch and then seeing the plate and eating it – it brings me a lot of joy," he says. "And it's improved my cooking so much. I'm eating healthily

now and trying out different things. I've never had Turkish food before, but that's my favourite now."

James now comes to a variety of different programmes at the Pantry and doesn't like to miss a demonstration or the opportunity to learn something new. "I was wasting a lot of food, but thanks to Cook for Good, I've learnt how to take leftovers and make them into another meal. I will also put herbs in my food now, which I never used to do." It also helped him recreate a dish his mother made in the days after Christmas: a bread pudding made of Christmas pudding. "That's been really special," he says.

The human interaction at Cook for Good has also helped bring him out of himself, and James is now volunteering doing gardening where he lives and has started interacting with neighbours more. He has even started attending the community meals, where members of Cook for Good share the food prepared by local companies during teambuilding activities. "It feels wonderful," he says. "Like you're part of something really unique."

While he may have struggled to directly ask for help to combat his loneliness, the Men's Grub Club helped – almost without him noticing – by encouraging him to get out of the house and try something completely different.

"I'm now coming out into the community more," he says. "Cook for Good does so much for the community, from the very young to the very old. There are people here from diverse backgrounds and different cultures, and everyone gets along. It's absolutely fantastic!"

James' mental health has also massively improved thanks to a major new addition to his life: his adopted cat, Mr. Jackson.

"He keeps me grounded, and I know I have someone else to look after now," he says. "I want to provide a nice home for him. I definitely feel less lonely than I was."

*Interview by Alexandra Topping*

# CREAMY PARSNIP AND PARMESAN SOUP

**Prep time:**
10 minutes

**Cooking time:**
1 hour

**Serves 4–6**

We first served this soup at our Christmas 2023 community meal, and it caused more excitement than the turkey-and-trimmings main course. Our 100 guests polished it off with gusto, and many took the recipe away to try at home over the holidays. It's a stunning take on the classic parsnip soup with its sweet richness enhanced by the addition of Parmesan cheese.

## INGREDIENTS

**1kg** parsnips

**2 tbsp** olive oil

**50g** Parmesan or Pecorino cheese

**1** onion

**2 tbsp** butter

**1.5 litres** vegetable or chicken stock

**4 tbsp** double cream (optional)

Salt and pepper

## METHOD

Preheat the oven to 200°C/Gas mark 6. Trim the parsnips, then cut them lengthways into halves or quarters, depending on their size. There's no need to peel them! Place the parsnips on a baking tray lined with non-stick baking paper and toss well with the olive oil to coat. Put in the oven and bake for 20 minutes.

Finely grate the cheese. Remove the parsnips from the oven, sprinkle with the cheese, then roast again for 15–20 minutes until golden brown.

Meanwhile, peel and chop the onion. Put a large saucepan or shallow casserole pan over a medium heat. Add the butter and melt. Add the chopped onion to the pan, stir, and cover with a lid. Cook until very soft, stirring occasionally, around 5 minutes. Add the roasted parsnips and any cheesy bits from the roasting tray to the pan. Add the stock, bring to the boil, cover, and then simmer for 10 minutes.

Once the soup has simmered, stir through the cream, if using, then blend until smooth. Taste and season with salt and pepper. Serve piping hot.

**TOP IT OFF**      Something herby is brilliant with this soup. Try crispy sage leaves, fresh thyme, or herb and garlic croutons.

**NO STRESS BREAD**      Warmed slices of our Portuguese water bread (which has a ciabatta-like texture) are gorgeous with this soup.

*See page 64 for soup image*

TOP: Creamy parsnip
and Parmesan soup

BOTTOM: Curried
parsnip soup

# CURRIED PARSNIP SOUP

**Prep time:**
10 minutes

**Cooking time:**
35 minutes

**Serves 4–6**

This mild curried soup is full of warm spices and the added creaminess of coconut milk. The squeeze of lime and scattering of coriander elevate it even further so don't be tempted to leave them out. It makes a delicious lunch but is also enough for an evening meal, especially with our easy homemade flatbreads on the side.

## INGREDIENTS

**2** onions

**4** garlic cloves

**2** apples
(Gala is our favourite variety)

**750g** parsnips

A small thumb of ginger
(approx. **5cm**)

**2 tbsp** olive oil

**1 tbsp** curry powder

**2 tsp** ground coriander

**½ tsp** turmeric

**1 litres** vegetable stock

**1 × 400ml** tin coconut milk

**½** lime

**20g** fresh coriander

Salt and pepper

## METHOD

Peel and finely chop the onions and garlic. Peel, core and roughly chop the apples. Peel and roughly chop the parsnips. Peel and finely grate the ginger.

Put a large saucepan or shallow casserole pan over a medium heat. Add the oil along with the onion. Sauté for 3–4 minutes, stirring constantly, until the onion starts to soften. Add the garlic, ginger, curry powder, ground coriander, turmeric, and apple. Lower the heat and sauté for a further 5–6 minutes until golden and fragrant.

Add the parsnips, vegetable stock, and a good pinch of salt. Stir well. Bring to the boil, cover, and simmer on a low heat until the parsnips are very tender, around 15 minutes.

Blend the mixture until very smooth. Juice the lime and add the lime juice along with the coconut milk. Taste and season with salt and pepper as needed. Finely chop the coriander and use it to garnish the soup.

## Prep time:
10 minutes

## Cooking time:
35 minutes

## Serves 4–6

# PEA, MINT, AND FETA SOUP

We have a pea-hater on our staff team, and this is the only way she will eat them: blended into this irresistibly smooth soup with creamy feta and cool mint. Don't be fooled by its apparent simplicity; it's got a sophisticated flavour that our Pantry members love. This is delicious served either hot or cold.

## INGREDIENTS

**1** large onion

**2** garlic cloves (optional)

**15g** mint

**2** medium floury or baking potatoes

**3 tbsp** olive oil

**800g** fresh or frozen peas

**1 litre** vegetable stock

**150ml** double cream

**100g** feta cheese

Salt and pepper

## METHOD

Peel and finely chop the onion and garlic, if using. Destem and finely chop the mint leaves (you can use the stems to make fresh mint tea). Peel and cut the potatoes into 1cm dice.

Set a large saucepan or shallow casserole pan on a medium heat. Add the olive oil followed by the onion and sauté until soft but not coloured. Add a pinch of salt. Add the garlic (if using) and potatoes and mix through. Cook for 5 minutes. Add the peas, mint, and vegetable stock. Season with salt and pepper.

Cook for 15 minutes until the potatoes are soft. When cooked, blend the soup until smooth and creamy. Stir in the double cream. Season with salt and pepper to taste. Gently reheat if serving hot or chill in the fridge for up to 3 days if you want to serve it cold.

Crumble the feta and sprinkle over the top of each bowl just before serving.

**TOP IT OFF**     If you have mint in abundance, add more to top it off. It's also lovely with a swirl of cream or yoghurt.

*See page 68 for soup image*

TOP: Mimi and Aya's
pea and artichoke soup

BOTTOM: Pea, mint
and feta soup

## INGREDIENTS

**1kg** slow-cooking cut of beef or lamb, we use brisket

**1** large onion

**4** garlic cloves

**3** carrots

**3** medium potatoes

**6** artichoke bottoms (or artichoke hearts)

A squeeze of lemon juice (if using fresh artichokes)

**75ml** olive oil

**1.5 litres** vegetable stock

**2 tbsp** tomato puree

**¼ tsp** ground cumin

**¼ tsp** turmeric

**¼ tsp** ras el hanout

**¼ tsp** ground ginger

**1** egg

**500g** fresh or frozen peas

**30g** fresh parsley

**30g** fresh coriander

Salt and pepper

# MIMI AND AYA'S PEA AND ARTICHOKE SOUP

Community Brigade graduate Mimi and her sister, Aya, cooked this soup for us one Wednesday when we were stacking our Pantry shelves. It's a traditional Algerian soup which has been passed down through their family. The story goes that in 1865, an Algerian couple planted peas and artichokes side by side in a barren field, and when the crops thrived, they decided to make them into soup.

## METHOD

Start by cutting your meat into 6 pieces. Peel and finely chop the onion and garlic. Peel and cut the carrots into 2cm dice. Peel the potatoes and cut each into 6 pieces. If using fresh artichokes, peel them to expose the bottoms, then wash them and place in water with a squeeze of lemon until required. Alternatively, drain tinned artichoke bottoms or hearts and rinse well. Cut the artichoke bottoms or hearts into halves.

Set a large saucepan or shallow casserole pan on a medium heat. Add 3 tablespoons of the oil followed by the potatoes. Cook until brown on all sides. Remove from the pan and set aside. Add some more oil to the pan to make it back up to 2 tablespoons. Add the meat and brown well on both sides. Add the onion, garlic, stock, and tomato puree, stir, and then cover. Reduce the heat slightly and cook for 10 minutes.

Uncover, add the spices, a good pinch of salt, and a good grinding of black pepper. Stir well, then cover again and cook for a further 10 minutes, stirring once or twice during this time. Add the browned potatoes along with the prepared carrot and artichokes to the pan. Stir, cover, and cook for 45 minutes.

Meanwhile, crack the egg into a bowl. Remove a couple of ladles of hot broth from the pan and add slowly to the egg, whisking as you add.

After 30 minutes have passed, check if the meat and vegetables are tender. If required, top up the stock and cook for a further 15–25 minutes until tender. Add the peas and bring back up to temperature. Chop the fresh herbs as the peas cook.

To finish the soup, slowly drizzle in the tempered egg while stirring continuously. Stir through the fresh herbs and serve.

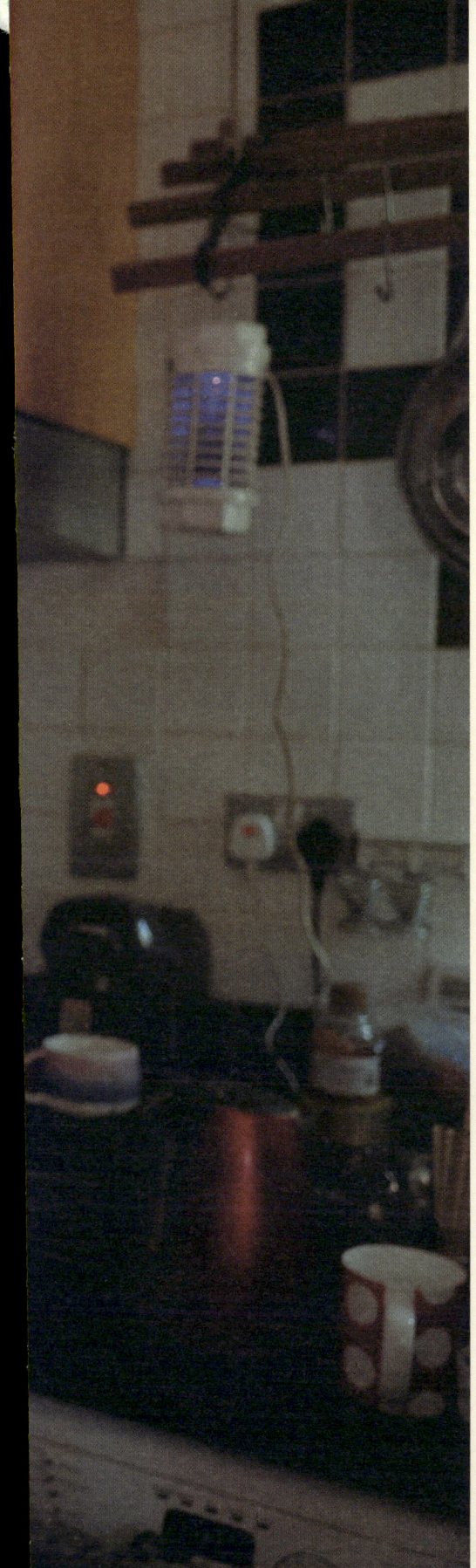

# REBECCA HENDERSON

"I'm someone who fought to get into the world," says Rebecca Henderson, sipping a cup of tea. "My mum was in labour for 42 hours, and I've just gone on fighting ever since."

Now 58, Rebecca recalls a childhood punctuated by bad health and headaches. "I was born with fluid on the brain, but they didn't actually discover I had hydrocephalus until I was 17," she says. When she hit puberty, she started suffering from nausea, blackouts, tremors, migraines, and bouts of vomiting.

"Finally, I was trying to do my A Levels, but I was found with my head on the desk, and I couldn't lift it up. Then they did an MRI scan on me." The doctors later told her that if she hadn't been operated on immediately, she would have had less than 12 hours to live.

But Rebecca never let the challenges she faced as a child get in her way, and she started working in the photographic industry. Always motivated to help others, she began volunteering at Disability Action in Islington and ended up working there for 16 years, despite having a stroke in her 30s. She then volunteered with Good Neighbours UK before also starting to volunteer at Cook for Good.

She describes herself as a "champion of people with visible impairments" and is always looking for ways to make their lives easier. She sometimes goes out with friends to speak to bar and club owners about how they can adapt their spaces to support people with epilepsy and other conditions. "People think that if you are not in a wheelchair, you aren't disabled and don't need help," she says. "But often, if you don't do something to help that person in a timely fashion, it will have a negative impact on the rest of their life."

Rebecca also calls herself the "bulldog" of the Pantry. She makes sure that everyone is taking their fair share and playing by the same rules. She appreciates that at the Pantry there is no us and them: everyone works together to make sure things run smoothly. "It's not austere here; the officialdom has been kind of taken out of it," she says. "If I say something to someone, I know they'll accept it from me. They'll think, 'she's one of us.'"

It is this sense of fair play running right through Cook for Good that makes her feel so at home, she says. "The whole ethos in this place is that there is a fair share for everyone: no one gets more, no one gets less," she says. "I love the camaraderie, the sense of purpose, the fairness, and just knowing that what we do here is addressing a huge need."

There is no means testing at Cook for Good; there is an acceptance of everyone, at all levels. "It's not patronising," she says. "Lots of people don't want to accept charity, but what we are doing is helping our members maximise what they've got."

In recent months, she has come to realise that, as well as helping, she may also be able to accept help. She now refers to herself as a "double agent": both a volunteer at Cook for Good and one of its members. "Yeah, I am proud. And if I can do it for myself, I do it for myself," she says. "But this place has also given me a kick up the bum. I do accept that, and I welcome it."

Rebecca's partner, Richard, died 12 years ago. He used to do all the cooking in their home as the impact of her stroke left her "a danger to herself" when holding a knife and lacking ideas and confidence in the kitchen. But now she has learned a raft of new skills. "It's been a learning curve. But I have to keep learning," she says, "because as soon as you stop learning, you're in a box."

Rebecca says that she has always found it hard to accept the label "disabled" but at Cook for Good she has learned to look at herself differently.

"If you look at the social model of disability, it's the removal of the barriers you need in order to access everyday services and manage your everyday life," she says. "If you own being disabled, you're not being a wimp, you're really not. You're just saying: put these things in place and then I can manage as well as anyone."

The sense of positivity and action at Cook for Good is infectious, she says. "I feel like this is not a charity; it's a resource. This place just allows people to make the most of what they have in life with the little funds that they've got."

*Interview by Alexandra Topping*

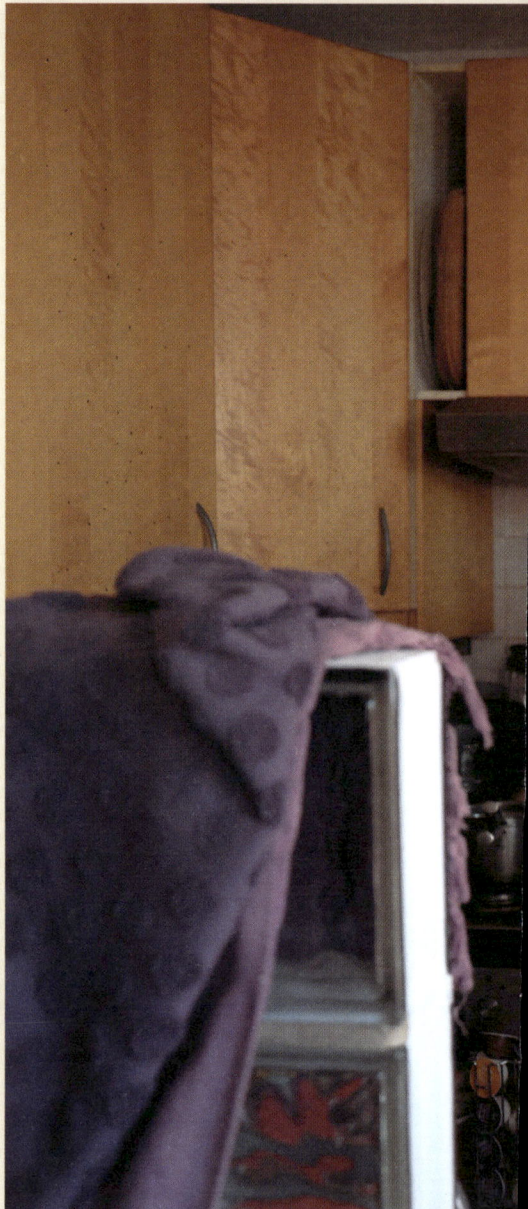

# DR JANE'S LENTIL, TOMATO, AND COCONUT DAHL

Jane Myat is a Camden GP who shares our interest in the positive impact of good food. She worked with our resident chef, Simone, to create Cook for Health, a community cooking course which supports diabetes patients to better manage their condition through healthy and joyful eating. She says: "I cook up large vats of this soup for community events and often get asked for the recipe. I like the way it borrows from lots of different cuisines – a bit like our community!"

## INGREDIENTS

**250g** red lentils

**1** carrot (or you can use a **200g** wedge of squash)

**2** large shallots or **6** smaller shallots

**2** garlic cloves

A **thumb** of ginger (approx. **5cm**)

**1** red chilli (more or less to taste)

**3 tbsp** coconut oil

**4** lime leaves

**2 tbsp** Madras curry powder

**1 × 400g** tinned tomatoes

**1 litre** water

**1 × 400g** tin coconut milk

**1** lemon

Salt and pepper

## METHOD

Wash and drain the lentils. Peel and finely dice the carrot or squash. Peel and finely dice the shallots, garlic, and ginger. Crush the ginger further in a pestle and mortar to release more juices and make a paste. Deseed and finely chop the chilli.

Set a large saucepan or shallow casserole pan on a medium heat. Add the oil followed by the shallots, garlic, chilli, and ginger. Gently sauté, without colouring. Once the vegetables are translucent, add the carrot and lime leaves and sweat for 5 minutes.

Add the curry powder and toast until aromatic. Add lentils and quickly fry with the shallots and spices. Add tomatoes and stir well. Cook for 3–4 minutes before adding the water and a generous pinch of salt, then simmer until the water is absorbed.

Add the coconut milk and continue to simmer for a further 3–4 minutes. Add lemon and season to taste. Remove lime leaves before serving.

**TOP IT OFF**     You can have a lot of fun with garnishes for this soup. Chopped or crushed roasted salted almonds or peanuts add a delicious crunch. Slow roasted cherry tomatoes or halved fresh tomatoes. A ripple of yoghurt gives a cool contrast. Fresh coriander, chilli flakes, and crispy onions are also enticing toppers.

*See page 76 for soup image*

TOP: Dr Jane's lentil, tomato, and coconut dahl

BOTTOM: Loved-by-all aromatic lentil soup

**Prep time:**
10 minutes

**Cooking time:**
40 minutes

**Serves 6**

*"I am desperate for autumn so I can make the spicy lentil soup again. Everyone – my kids, my 90-year-old parents – LOVES this soup."*
Jane Garvey, Broadcaster

# LOVED-BY-ALL AROMATIC LENTIL SOUP

Our team absolutely love this soup; in fact, the first time one of them took the recipe home to try, she ate it for lunch every day for a week. Warming and nourishing, it's packed full of protein and spices. Although it's deliciously creamy, the chilli and mustard seeds add a gentle kick that will help blow the cobwebs away. If you like smooth soups, you might want to blend it, but we tend to serve it as it comes with some flatbread or naan. Don't forget to squeeze in the lemon at the end – it's an absolute must.

## INGREDIENTS

**1** onion

**2** mild red chillies

**1** tomato

**200g** red lentils

**2** garlic cloves

A small **thumb** of ginger

**2 tbsp** olive oil

**1 tsp** black mustard seeds

**1 tsp** Baharat or Lebanese **7**-spice

**½ tsp** ground turmeric

**1 litre** vegetable stock

**1 × 400ml** tin coconut milk

**1** lemon

Salt and pepper

## METHOD

Finely chop the onion. Deseed and finely chop the chillies. Dice the tomato into small cubes. Wash and drain the lentils. Peel and finely grate the garlic and the ginger to make a paste.

Set a large saucepan or shallow casserole pan on a medium heat. Coat with a thin layer of the oil. Add the mustard seeds and fry for 2 minutes until they start to pop. Stir in the onion, garlic, ginger, chillies, Baharat/7-spice, and turmeric. Sauté until the onion begins to turn light brown. Add in the diced tomato and sauté until they soften. Add the lentils, coconut milk, vegetable stock, and a good pinch of salt and simmer over a medium heat for 20–25 minutes until thickened and the lentils are cooked. Add the juice from the lemon, starting with the juice of half and then adding more to taste. Season with salt and pepper to taste.

To serve, either blend the soup or leave it as it is for more texture. Garnish with your choice of tasty toppings.

**TOP IT OFF**     We love this soup capped with swirl of Greek yoghurt, crispy onions, and fresh coriander leaves. It's also fun with a sprinkling of Bombay mix or a spicy drizzle of chilli oil.

**NO STRESS BREAD**     This soup is incredible when paired with our sundried tomato and feta focaccia. It's the perfect way to turn a simple store-cupboard soup into a hearty meal.

# MUSHROOM AND WILD RICE SOUP

This is one of Karen's favourite soups. She brought it in for everyone to try, and it's now a Pantry regular. If you're a fan of mushroom risotto, this is the soup for you: luxurious, earthy, and so delicious. You can make it with either wild or brown rice, as both will give it that wholesome nutty flavour. It's so substantial that it almost doesn't need bread with it – but if you want to sneak some focaccia on the side, we won't tell.

## INGREDIENTS

**1** large onion

**3** garlic cloves

**1** large carrot

**1** celery stick

**285g** chestnut mushrooms

**2 tbsp** olive oil

**2 tbsp** butter

**225g** wild rice, or rice mix with wild rice

**1 tbsp** herbs de Provence

**1.5 litres** vegetable stock

**175ml** double cream

**50g** Parmesan or Pecorino cheese

Salt and pepper

### GARNISH

**120g** chestnut mushrooms

**1** garlic clove

**25g** flat-leaf parsley

**1 tbsp** olive oil

Salt

## METHOD

Peel and finely chop the onion and garlic. Peel and cut the carrot into 1cm dice. Cut the celery into 1cm dice. Wipe and then finely slice the mushrooms.

Put a large saucepan or shallow casserole pan over a medium heat. Add the oil and butter. Add the onion, carrot, and celery to the pan and cook for 6–8 minutes until softened but not coloured. Increase the heat to medium-high and add the mushrooms and garlic. Continue to cook for another 8 minutes, stirring occasionally, until the mushrooms are soft and slightly coloured.

Add the rice to the pan and stir to coat. Cook for 1–2 minutes before adding the herbs de Provence. Season with a generous pinch of salt and a good grinding of pepper. Add the vegetable stock, cover, and bring to the boil. Then simmer for around 45 minutes or until the rice is tender.

Meanwhile, make the garnish. Wipe and finely slice the chestnut mushrooms. Peel and finely chop the garlic. Finely chop the parsley. Set a frying pan over a medium heat. Add the olive oil, followed by the sliced mushrooms, and fry until they are tender and golden brown. Add the garlic and a pinch of salt and continue to cook for another minute, stirring constantly. Set aside for garnish.

Once the rice is cooked, remove the lid to the pan and stir through the cream. Finely grate the cheese and stir into the soup until well combined. Serve hot garnished with the sautéed mushrooms and a sprinkling of chopped parsley.

*See page 80 for soup image*

TOP: Cream of mushroom soup

BOTTOM: Mushroom and wild rice soup

# CREAM OF MUSHROOM SOUP

Not to be confused with the tinned version, this is a smooth, velvety delight that's packed with goodness. Our community love to give us feedback on the soups we serve, and for this one they suggested adding extra milk or cream to lighten the colour. In the unlikely event that you have any left over, it makes a great sauce poured over a bowl of pasta or some roasted chicken.

## INGREDIENTS

**800g** chestnut mushrooms

**2** medium onions

**2** garlic cloves

**2 tbsp** olive oil

**2 tbsp** butter

**¾ tsp** dried or fresh tarragon

**1 litre** vegetable or chicken stock

**100ml** double cream

Salt and pepper

## METHOD

Wipe the mushrooms and trim off any tough stalk ends. Roughly chop or slice. Peel and finely chop the onions and garlic.

Set a large saucepan or shallow casserole pan on a medium heat. Add the olive oil and butter. When hot, add the mushrooms and sauté until they are lightly browned, around 10 minutes. Add the chopped onion and garlic and mix well. Lower the heat and gently cook until the onions are soft but not coloured.

Add the stock, tarragon, and a good pinch of salt to the pan and bring to a simmer. Cook uncovered for 10 minutes. Remove from the heat.

Blend until smooth. Return the soup to a low heat and add more stock or water if it's too thick for your taste. Stir in the cream and a generous amount of freshly ground black pepper. Season with salt and pepper to taste.

**TOP IT OFF**     We love to top it off with a good pinch of finely chopped parsley and a little swirl of cream.

**NO STRESS BREAD**     Amel's matlou-a is the perfect bread for this creamy, dreamy soup.

# USE IT UP

One of the many joys of soup is that it can get you out of having to go to the shops. It's so versatile that you can assemble something tasty using the odds and ends from your fridge or freezer. And if, like us, you're trying to waste less food, it's an easy way to use up slightly tired veg, yesterday's leftovers, or that jar of spices you bought for a specific recipe and haven't touched since. Here are some gorgeous soups using ingredients that often end up getting thrown away.

# SUNDAY ROAST SOUP

**Prep time:**
15 minutes

**Cooking time:**
45 minutes

**Serves 4–6**

We run a community cooking class called Loving your Leftovers, and this recipe just about sums up the principle behind it. It's the ultimate way to make sure none of your Sunday roast gets thrown in the bin. Simply take whatever meat, veg, and potatoes you have left, chuck in some stock, seasoning, and a few extras like peas and carrots, and then cook it all up together. If you've got some leftover gravy to stir in towards the end, so much the better.

## INGREDIENTS

**2** onions

**2** garlic cloves

**2** carrots

**1** celery stick

**2** medium Maris Piper potatoes or leftover roast potatoes

**200g** leftover roast meat (chicken, turkey, lamb, pork, or beef)

**1 tbsp** olive oil

**3** sprigs thyme or rosemary

**1.5 litres** vegetable, chicken, or beef stock

**200g** fresh or frozen peas

**300g** leftover green vegetables (e.g., Brussel sprouts, cabbage, green beans)

**2–4 tbsp** leftover gravy (optional)

Salt and pepper

## METHOD

Peel and finely chop the onions and garlic. Peel and chop the carrots into 1cm dice. Cut the celery into 1cm dice. If you don't have any roast potatoes left over, peel and chop raw potatoes into 2cm dice. Shred the cooked meat off the bone.

Set a large saucepan or shallow casserole pan on a medium heat. Add the oil and, once warm, stir in the onions and cook until soft but not coloured. Add the garlic, carrot, and celery. Tie the herbs into a bundle with string or strip the leaves and finely chop. Stir the herbs through, and cook for a further 5–10 minutes until fragrant and starting to soften.

If using raw potatoes, stir them in now. Then add the stock and bring to the boil. Cover, lower the heat, and simmer until the vegetables are tender, around 15–20 minutes.

Finally, add the peas, leftover green vegetables, leftover roast potatoes (if using) and shredded leftover meat to the pan and stir to combine. If you have any leftover gravy, add that too. Season with salt and pepper to taste, then leave to cook for 5 minutes.

You can eat the soup as it is, or if you prefer a smoother soup blend all the veg before adding the meat and stir in the leftover shredded meat right at the end, gently warming before serving.

# MIXED VEGETABLE SOUP

This is the soup that proves that you can make something amazing without a fixed recipe; if you've got the basic principles in mind, you can make it with whatever is lurking in your fridge. It's all about having the confidence to improvise with what you have to hand: add rice, lentils, or pasta and switch up the herbs. You can't go wrong, and you might develop a new favourite along the way.

## METHOD

Peel and finely chop the onion and garlic. Peel and chop the carrot into 1cm dice. Chop the celery into 1cm dice. Chop the surplus vegetables into equal sized pieces.

Set a large saucepan or shallow casserole pan on a medium heat. Add the oil and/or butter. Once warm and melted, add the onion and cook until soft but not coloured. Add the garlic, carrot, celery, and dried spices/herbs and cook for a further 5 minutes until fragrant and starting to soften.

Add the remaining vegetables and stir well. Soften, stirring regularly, for a few minutes. Add the stock, fresh herbs, and legumes/grains that can be blended in (such as red lentils) and bring to a boil, then simmer the soup until the vegetables are tender, around 20 minutes. If you want to add grains or legumes without blending them in (e.g., barley, pasta, rice), cook them separately and add after the initial cooking and blending of the vegetables.

Once cooked, blend the soup or leave chunky, according to choice. Stir in the cream or coconut milk (optional) and season to taste with salt and pepper.

**Prep time:**
15 minutes

**Cooking time:**
25–40 minutes

**Serves 4–6**

## INGREDIENTS

**1** onion

**1** carrot

**1** celery stick

**2** garlic cloves

**1kg** surplus vegetables

**1 tbsp** olive oil

**1 tbsp** butter (or swap with olive oil for vegan)

Dried herbs and/or spices of choice

**1.5 litres** vegetable stock

Surplus fresh herbs of choice

Surplus grains or legumes of choice

**150ml** cream or coconut milk (optional)

Salt and pepper

❝ I love exploring different flavours and had to stop due to financial hardship. The Pantry has helped me regain some of that. ❞

*Pantry member*

# MARY HARVEY

The King's Cross Mary Harvey lived in the 1980s was a very different place from the upscale business and leisure zone that people know today. The 76-year-old remembers that she didn't have a telephone in the house; instead, she would use the pay phone a few minutes' walk away. But the area was known for problems with soliciting, and "as a woman you couldn't walk down the road without men in cars propositioning you," she recalls. "It didn't feel like a safe place at all."

Yet Mary's memories from that time are happy. Her boys were teenagers and would play with their friends in the streets before all piling back to her house for dinner. "Sometimes there would be 16 children over," she reminisces. "They all loved coming to our house."

She worked the night shift packing shelves in Sainsbury's, while her husband worked days as a bus driver. Without mobile phones, they often left each other notes in the house. "Our notes were the best; they were nice," she says. "I suppose they were love notes. We were happy."

Mary sits with her beautifully brushed hair surrounding her face like a shining silver curtain in the light-filled Cook for Good Pantry on the Priory Green Estate. She still lives close by.

She explains that after her husband retired, he became ill and life got harder. Her younger son died, Mary suffered a back injury, and she started looking after her grandchild. She became more isolated. "I used to walk my grandson to school every day, walk back, and then pick him up at half past three, and I never had a soul to say hello to," she recalls. "I didn't know anybody. I never had any friends. I used to lock myself away a bit."

Then, she saw an advert for Cook for Good cooking classes and thought she could help her grandson by learning to cook healthier food. Walking into the Pantry for the first time took all the courage she could muster: "I walked up and down I don't know how many times, trying to get the confidence to come in."

Unlike many of the other people who come to the Pantry, she freely admits that she has no interest in cooking at all. "I haven't got a good relationship with food; me and food don't get on," she says. And becoming part of life in the Pantry two years ago hasn't really changed that, she confesses, even if she does sometimes help to make the communal soup that members enjoy when they visit. But it has given her something else: a new sense of purpose, a new set of friends, a new lease of life.

She describes being welcomed into the fold by Community Manager, Martha Ahmet, who asked what she was good at, insisting that everyone was good at something. "I said 'well, my son-in-law says I make a good cup of tea!'" She adds, "I can honestly say, and I really, really mean this, that was the start of a new life for me."

Mary has since become a vital part of the Cook for Good volunteering team, helping prepare its weekly surplus food pantry, where members pay £3.50 each week to choose a basket of food worth between £30 and £35. She takes pride in making sure that the produce looks neat and inviting to the members who come in to browse.

"I think the main thing for me was that when I started coming to Cook for Good, I would see people on the school run or get on the bus and people would say 'Hello Mary, you okay?' I would wonder how they knew my name, and then I'd remember that it was because of the Pantry. It was just really lovely."

She's also found help in other ways. Her grandson is autistic, and on one occasion a psychologist came to the Pantry to help carers like Mary understand the condition better. "The lady spoke to me one-on-one and helped me so much," she says.

But as well as the practical help, Mary thinks that being part of the Cook for Good community has also given her a new sense of her place in the world. "I wasn't just Nan anymore," she explains, "I wasn't just Great-Nan, I was Mary. And that felt really nice."

And when her husband recently passed away, she realised that she no longer felt lonely; she had found a new place to belong where people wanted to help support her through her grief: "This is another family. We all have our ups and downs, but it's a family that cares."

*Interview by Alexandra Topping*

**Prep time:**
10 minutes

**Cooking time:**
40 minutes

**Serves 4–6**

## INGREDIENTS

**1** large onion

**1** large potato

**1** lime

**800g** sweetcorn kernels (frozen or tinned)

**2 tbsp** vegetable oil

**1 ½ tsp** smoked paprika

**¾ tsp** ground cumin

**1.25 litre** vegetable stock

Salt and pepper

### GARNISH

**1** green chilli

**100g** feta cheese

### TOP IT OFF
For additional texture and some crunch, you can top the soup with crumbled tortilla chips.

### NO STRESS BREAD
Try this soup with warm, buttered slices of our delicious cornbread.

# MEXICAN SWEETCORN SOUP

We often have tins of sweetcorn left on our Pantry shelves. This recipe, which we devised to help shift them, has our members queueing up for seconds and is a favourite of our team-building clients too. It's a gorgeous thick broth, simple and tasty, with smoky flavours of paprika and charred sweetcorn that really hit the spot. The feta is optional, but we highly recommend including it if you can as it adds a layer of creaminess that is hard to beat.

## METHOD

Peel and finely chop the onion. Peel and cut the potato into 1cm dice. Juice half of the lime and set aside. Slice the other half thinly and set aside for garnish. Drain the tins of sweetcorn.

Set a large saucepan or shallow casserole pan on a medium heat. Add 1 tbsp oil to the pan and, once warm, add the drained or defrosted sweetcorn. Cook undisturbed for 2–3 minutes so the kernels turn golden on the bottom. Stir, spread out again, and repeat until the sweetcorn is golden and charred in spots. Transfer the sweetcorn into a bowl.

Reduce the heat to medium and add the remaining oil to the pan. Add the onion and potatoes and cook for 3–4 minutes until softened and a pale golden. Add the spices, cook for a further minute or two, and then add the stock.

Put 5 tbsp of the sweetcorn into a small bowl and set aside. Add the rest back to the pan. Bring to the boil and then reduce the heat to a simmer. Cover and cook for 5–10 minutes until the potato is fully softened.

While the soup is cooking, prepare the garnish. Thinly slice the chillies and crumble the feta.

Remove the soup from the heat and squeeze in the lime juice. Blend the soup until smooth. Season to taste with salt and pepper. Add more stock or water if the soup is too thick.

Garnish the warm soup with the reserved sweetcorn and the feta, chillies, and lime slices. Sprinkle with a little more smoked paprika.

# CREAM OF SPINACH SOUP

**Prep time:**
10 minutes

**Cooking time:**
40 minutes

**Serves 4–6**

Our Pantry is a real family affair: members with young children tend to bring them along, and they tuck into the soup as heartily as their parents do. This soup is really popular with our younger visitors and a great way to get this leafy superfood into their diets. We've tried it with both fresh and frozen leftover spinach, and it got devoured in equal measure. Creamy, healthy, and delicious, all in one bowl.

## INGREDIENTS

**500g** frozen spinach

**1** large onion

**2** garlic cloves

**1** large potato

**1 tbsp** olive oil

**1 tbsp** butter

**150ml** double cream

**50ml** milk

Freshly grated nutmeg

**1.25 litres** vegetable stock

Salt and pepper

## METHOD

Defrost the spinach and drain off any excess water. Peel and finely chop the onion and garlic. Peel and cut the potato into 2cm dice.

Put a large saucepan or shallow casserole pan over a low heat. Add the butter and oil followed by the onion and garlic. Sweat until soft but not coloured – add a little salt during this stage. Add the cream, milk, and a pinch of grated nutmeg and bring to the boil. When at boiling point, add the spinach, potato, and stock. Cook until the potato is soft.

Cool slightly and blend until completely smooth. Season with salt and pepper to taste.

**TOP IT OFF**     For an added hit of delicious green goodness, finish with herb oil, a swirl of cream, and garlic and herb croutons.

# TUSCAN BREAD SOUP

**Prep time:**
10 minutes

**Cooking time:**
40 minutes

**Serves 4–6**

Known in Italy as Ribollita, this is a fantastic way to use up stale bread (which tops the charts as one of the UK's most wasted foods), and you can swap the cavolo nero for any other dark green veg you have in your fridge too. Not only is it delicious, but this soup is also particularly good for vegetarians as the beans are a great source of veggie-friendly protein.

## INGREDIENTS

**1** brown onion

**1** small red onion

**1** garlic clove

**2** carrots

**2** celery sticks

**1** leek

**200g** butternut squash

**200g** cavolo nero (or other dark kale)

**1 × 400g** tin cannellini beans

**200g** stale bread

**2 tbsp** olive oil

**1** bay leaf

**¼ tsp** fennel seeds

**¼ tsp** chilli flakes

**1 × 400g** tin chopped tomatoes

**1** Parmesan rind (optional but tasty!)

**500ml** vegetable stock

Salt and pepper

### GARNISH

**2 tbsp** extra virgin olive oil

**60g** Parmesan or Pecorino cheese (optional)

**25g** parsley

## METHOD

Peel and finely chop the onions and garlic. Peel and cut the carrots into 1cm dice. Cut the celery into 1cm dice. Wash and trim the leek and cut into ½ cm rounds. Peel and deseed the butternut squash and cut into 2cm chunks. Cut the cavolo nero into thin shreds. Tear the bread into chunks.

Blend half the tinned beans together with all the liquid from the can into a loose puree.

Set a large saucepan or shallow casserole pan on a medium heat. Add the oil followed by the onions and garlic. Sauté for 6–7 minutes until softened. Add the carrot, celery, and bay leaf together with a pinch of salt and cook for a further 5 minutes. Stir in the fennel seeds and chilli flakes and cook until fragrant. Add the leek, squash, and cavolo nero. Stir well, then cover and cook for 10 minutes, stirring occasionally.

Add the tinned tomatoes, pureed beans, cheese rind (if using), and stock. Cover again and simmer for up to 40 minutes until all the vegetables are tender. Stir through the remaining cannellini beans and the bread and cook for a further 5 minutes.

Meanwhile, finely chop the parsley for garnish. To serve, drizzle with olive oil and sprinkle over the grated cheese, if using. Place under the grill until crisp and then scatter over the parsley.

**NO STRESS BREAD**     To help further mop up the sunny flavours of this Italian soup, pair it with our black olive and caramelised onion focaccia. (Any leftover bread can be used to make another batch of soup!)

# GREEN GODDESS SOUP

An immune system booster that's packed full of flavour. You can use any green vegetables that you have in your fridge or freezer so feel free to experiment, and if you want to make it vegan, swap the cream for dairy-free alternatives or just leave it out. We love this soup's fresh green colour and the fact that it does you good as well as tasting good. We serve it regularly when we get to cough and cold season.

## INGREDIENTS

**1** onion

**4** garlic cloves

**1** leek (white part only)

**1** medium bulb fennel

**3** celery sticks

**1** potato

**1** head broccoli

**150g** kale

**2 tbsp** olive oil, plus
extra for drizzling

**¾ tsp** ground allspice

**¾ tsp** ground cumin or coriander

**1.25 litres** water or vegetable stock

**200g** frozen or fresh peas

**200g** spinach leaves

**180ml** double cream

Salt and pepper

## METHOD

Peel and finely chop the onion and garlic. Wash the leek and thinly slice. Cut the fennel and celery into 1cm dice. Peel and cut the potato into 2cm cubes. Cut any hard parts away from the broccoli stalk and then cut the florets and stalk into 2cm pieces. Strip the leaves from the kale. Roughly chop the leaves and finely chop the stalks (discard any really woody stalks).

Set a large saucepan or shallow casserole pan on a medium heat. Add the oil followed by the onion, garlic, leek, fennel, and celery. Cook for 5–10 minutes until softened. Add in the spices and cook for another minute or until aromatic. Add the water or stock, potato, broccoli, and kale. Season with salt and pepper. Stir, bring to a gentle simmer, and cook for 10–12 minutes or until the potato is tender.

Take the pan off the heat and add the peas and spinach. Blend until as smooth as possible. Stir in the cream right before serving.

**TOP IT OFF**     Amplify the goodness of this delicious green soup by finishing it off with toasted seeds and a drizzle of olive oil.

**NO STRESS BREAD**     Our wholegrain seeded loaf, sliced and lightly buttered, is the perfect partner for this nourishing soup.

# BROCCOLI STALK SOUP

**Prep time:**
15 minutes

**Cooking time:**
40 minutes

**Serves 4–6**

We run regular Use It Up cooking classes and demos to help our community feel more confident about using food – or parts of food – that might otherwise be thrown away. This recipe is a classic example, turning the unloved broccoli stalk into the star of the show. It produces a lighter colour and nuttier flavour than using the head of the broccoli but is every bit as delicious and so cost-effective.

## INGREDIENTS

**1** onion

**2** garlic cloves

**1** small leek

**1** celery stick

**500g** broccoli stalks

**375g** potatoes

**2 tbsp** olive oil

**2 tbsp** butter

**1.5–2 litres** vegetable stock

**100ml** double cream

½ lemon

Salt and pepper

## METHOD

Peel and finely chop the onion and garlic. Clean the leek, discard the toughest part of the green leaves, and then roughly chop the rest. Cut the celery into 1cm dice. Trim just the very toughest part of the broccoli stalks and cut the remainder of the stalks into 2cm dice. Peel the potatoes and cut into 2cm dice.

Set a large saucepan or shallow casserole pan on a medium heat. Add the oil and butter. Once the butter is melted, add the onion, and cook until soft but not coloured. Add the garlic, leek, and celery and cook for a further 5 minutes or until fragrant and starting to soften.

Add 1.5 litres of vegetable stock followed by the broccoli stalks and potatoes. Bring to a boil and then reduce the heat to simmer the soup until the broccoli and potatoes are tender. Once cooked, blend the soup until very smooth, adding more stock, if needed.

Stir in the cream and season to taste with salt, pepper, and a good squeeze of lemon juice.

**TOP IT OFF** Wonderful with a swirl of cream and the crunchy finish of garlic and herb croutons.

# SAFIA HASSAN

Safia Hassan has spent most of her life looking after, nurturing, and educating children: five of her own, two of her nieces, her grandchildren, and countless others during her time as an early years educator.

"I've loved it," says the 56-year-old. "The thing with children is that you can see tomorrow what you taught them today. And they are hilarious. In how many jobs can you know that you will go to work every morning and they will crack you up?"

But after many years, she has decided that she wants to pursue a new career and take a different path – and that all started when she took a knife skills class at Cook for Good.

"I didn't know what I was looking for," she says about her decision to join the community. "I walked in, I had no plan, nothing. But by the end of my first session here I wanted to become a profession-al cook, I had a business plan, and I had a name: Safia's Spices."

A lover of street food and an avid fan of London's many different cuisines, Safia noted that few people knew the food culture of the country where she was born. "You can see everything in the world here, but you don't see Somali restaurants very often. When I eat my food, I am transported, and I want to bring that experience to others."

Safia arrived in the UK from Somalia at the age of 15 to join her father, who was working on ships out of the docks of Liverpool. When she was 19, her family moved to London, where she met her husband, had children, and started work.

She worked as a teaching assistant around her children's school hours. Then, in her 40s and a single mother of five, she took the plunge to do a degree, specialising in early years education. More recently, after decades of looking after others, she walked through the doors of Cook for Good and realised that she wanted to do something just for herself.

"I've always loved food, but being here made me realise that I wanted a change and to go into catering," she says. "I would say that for the first time I am doing this for me, not for anyone else. My children come first, and they are the love of my life, but this is for Safia. I want it to succeed, but the main goal is just to see if I can do it."

She has now completed food safety courses and learned about sauce making and fish preparation. Recently she completed a successful two-week stint of work experience with Genuine

Dining, working in huge multinational companies like Spotify, which she describes as an exhilarating learning experience.

"I was comfortable with front of house jobs like serving people. I can transfer the experience I have had working in schools, but I really wanted to learn what the chef actually does in the kitchen," she says. "That was quite an eye-opener for me."

For Safia, food is the great leveller and the secret to Cook for Good's success in bringing people together from all walks of life. "There is no racism or judgement in food," she says. "If it tastes good to you, that only has to do with your palate. It's a different language, and it helps us connect."

In Somalia, hospitality and welcoming people into your home are incredibly important, she explains. "And when you share food with people, you are saying you respect that person, you want to get to know them, you want to welcome them into your home. It's getting to know people on a deeper level – and that is what happens here."

Her dream now is to have a stall selling authentic Somali food. "I want to see people eating; I want them to enjoy themselves," she says. "I want to put my food on the map, and hopefully we will expand from there."

Making these plans would not have been possible had she not walked through the doors of Cook for Good, she says. "It has built up my confidence and has given me the skills. If the whole team had not made me feel welcome, given me kindness and the education and experience, I would not have been able to say I can do this; but now... I feel I can."

*Interview by Alexandra Topping*

# GAZPACHO

**Prep time:**
15 minutes, plus minimum
1 hour (or up to 24 hours)
marinating

**Cooking time:**
5 minutes

**Serves 4–6**

A classic chilled soup that's adored by us all, but particularly our Community Manager, Martha. She grew up in Spain and tells us it's a staple of every Andalusian kitchen in the summer. The secret is to use the ripest tomatoes you can get – if they're over-ripe, so much the better – so it's a brilliant way to use up any that you have lurking in the fridge. We served this in shot glasses to celebrate the opening of the Community Kitchen, and it went down a storm.

## INGREDIENTS

**2kg** very ripe vine tomatoes (over-ripe best)

**1** green pepper

**2** medium red onions

**1** cucumber

**4** garlic cloves

**120g** white or sourdough bread

**4 tbsp** sherry vinegar or red/white wine vinegar

**4 tbsp** olive oil

Salt and pepper

A handful of ice

A pinch of sugar, if needed

### GARNISH

½ red onion

½ green pepper

¼ cucumber

**20** pitted black olives

**2** hard-boiled eggs

## METHOD

Core and roughly chop the tomatoes. Core and roughly chop the green pepper. Peel and roughly chop the onions. Roughly chop the cucumber. Peel and finely chop the garlic. Put all the chopped vegetables into a large mixing bowl.

Remove the crusts from the bread and cut into chunks. Add the vinegar, olive oil, and bread to the vegetables. Season well with salt and pepper. Mix thoroughly and leave for as long as possible to marinate (minimum 1 hour at room temperature, up to overnight in the fridge).

Finely chop all the ingredients for the garnish and mix in a small bowl.

Once marinated, blend all the soup ingredients together until smooth. If serving immediately add a handful of ice before blending to help chill the soup down quickly. Check the seasoning and, if necessary, add salt, pepper, olive oil, or vinegar. If the soup is very acidic, add a little sugar.

Serve the soup chilled topped with the garnish.

**Prep time:**
10 minutes

**Cooking time:**
1 hour 15 minutes

**Serves 4–6**

# NOT-QUITE-FRENCH ONION SOUP

This is a soup worth taking time over: the longer you let the onions caramelise, the sweeter it will taste. So put on some tunes or a podcast and let the heat and the ingredients work their magic. One member of our team swears by adding a teaspoon of Marmite to give it a dash of sweet saltiness – it may not be the traditional French way, but it's absolutely delicious. And whatever you do, don't leave out the cheesy croutons.

## INGREDIENTS

**6** large red or white onions

**2** garlic cloves

**25g** parsley

**4 tbsp** olive oil

**2 tbsp** butter

**1 tsp** caster sugar

**125ml** white wine

**2 litres** of beef or veg stock

**1 tbsp** fresh thyme leaves

**2** bay leaves

**1 tbsp** brandy (optional)

Salt and pepper

### GARNISH

**1** French stick or baguette

**2 tbsp** olive oil

**150g** Gruyere cheese

**1 tbsp** Parmesan or Pecorino cheese

## METHOD

Peel and thinly slice the onions. Peel and finely chop the garlic. Finely chop the parsley.

Put a large saucepan or shallow casserole pan on a medium heat. Add 3 tablespoons of the oil along with the onion and stir well. Cook the onion for 10–15 minutes or until nicely softened.

Increase the heat to medium-high. Add the remaining tablespoon of oil together with the butter. Cook, stirring regularly, until the onions start to brown, around 30–40 minutes. Sprinkle with the sugar and a generous pinch of salt. Continue to cook for a further 10 minutes until the onions are very brown. Add the garlic and cook for one more minute.

Deglaze the pan by adding the white wine. Scrape all the brown bits from the bottom of the pan. Add the stock, thyme, and bay leaves and bring to the boil. Cover the pan, lower the heat, and simmer for 30 minutes. Season to taste with salt and pepper. Remove the bay leaves. If using brandy, add towards the end of the cooking.

To make the croutons, cut the French stick on the angle into slices of around 1.5cm thick. Brush the bread generously with olive oil on both sides and then toast in the oven until lightly browned. Finely grate the Gruyere and Parmesan or Pecorino and mix the cheeses together. Turn the toasts over and sprinkle with grated cheese. Return to the oven and bake until bubbly and lightly browned.

To serve, ladle the soup into bowls and place one or two croutons on top of each portion. Sprinkle with chopped parsley.

# EBRIMA'S GAMBIAN SOUP

*Donated by Houston & Hawkes*

**Prep time:**
25 minutes

**Cooking time:**
55 minutes

**Serves 4–6**

We met Houston & Hawkes through a mutual Kings Cross connection who recognised that their principles as a B Corp business were perfectly aligned with ours. Now one of our culinary partners, they support us in a variety of ways, including sharing both chefs and clients with us. This vibrant soup has been created for us by Ebrima Kibbeh, one of their junior chefs, inspired by the flavours of his Gambian heritage.

## INGREDIENTS

**350g** courgettes

**700g** beetroot

**400g** plantain

**1** onion

**500g** sweet potato

**250g** asparagus

**120ml** vegetable oil

**1.5 litres** vegetable stock

**1 tsp** paprika

**3 tbsp** coconut milk

Salt and pepper

## METHOD

Trim and cut the courgettes into 2cm dice. Scrub the beetroot clean (or peel) and cut into 2cm dice. Peel the plantain and thinly slice. Peel and finely dice the onion. Peel and cut the sweet potato into 2cm dice. Trim the woody ends from the asparagus and discard. Cut the tips off and set aside for the garnish. Cut the remainder of the stems into 1cm slices at an angle, giving you elongated slices for the garnish.

Set a large saucepan or shallow casserole dish over a medium heat. Add 1 tablespoon of the vegetable oil followed by the onion and paprika. Sauté for 6–8 minutes, until starting to soften. Fold in all the courgette and beetroot to the pan, half of the plantain, and half of the sweet potato. Cook for 10 minutes or until the vegetables start to colour.

Pour in the stock and cover with a lid. Turn the heat down and simmer for 30 minutes or until all the veg is tender. Blend the soup until smooth. Add salt and pepper to taste.

To make the garnish, add the remaining vegetable oil to a frying pan (or enough to create a shallow, 1cm-deep layer). Heat on medium-high until hot and then add the reserved plantain, sweet potato, and elongated asparagus slices (save the tips to fry separately). Fry until golden brown and crispy. Remove with a slotted spoon onto kitchen paper to drain. Finally, add the asparagus tips and fry until starting to colour – these will cook quicker than the stems.

Stir the coconut milk through the soup and then heat gently before serving. Serve garnished with the fried vegetables.

**Prep time:**
10 minutes

**Cooking time:**
1 hour

**Serves 4–6**

# ASPARAGUS SOUP WITH LEMON AND PARMESAN

A stunning combination of ingredients that will give your taste buds a treat: the freshness of asparagus, the zestiness of lemons, and the earthy richness of Parmesan, all in one bowl. The soup is delightfully light and a brilliant way to make the most of asparagus season – if you've already used the tips in a different recipe, this works equally well just with leftover spears. For a flavour boost, add a Parmesan rind to the soup as it's simmering and remove it just before blending.

## INGREDIENTS

**2** bunches asparagus (approx. **1** kg)

**3 tbsp** butter

**2** onions

**3** garlic cloves

**1.4 litres** vegetable or chicken stock

½ lemon

**50g** Parmesan or Pecorino cheese, plus extra for garnish

Salt and pepper

## METHOD

Trim the woody ends from the asparagus and discard. Trim the tops from one of the bunches of asparagus and set aside for garnish. Cut the remaining tips and spears into 2cm pieces. Peel and chop the onions and garlic.

Set a large saucepan or shallow casserole pan on a medium heat. Add the butter and, once melted, stir in the onions and garlic and cook for 6–8 minutes until soft and translucent. Add the chopped asparagus to the pan along with the stock, one teaspoon of salt, and a good grinding of black pepper. Bring to the boil, then cover and turn down the heat to low. Simmer for 30 minutes until the asparagus are tender.

Meanwhile, bring a small pan of salted water to the boil. Cook the reserved asparagus tips for a few minutes until tender but still crisp. Drain the tips then throw into very cold (or iced) water to refresh. When cool, drain and set aside.

Blend the soup with a stick blender or in a food processor in batches until completely smooth. Juice the half lemon. Bring the soup back to a simmer and stir through the lemon juice. Finely grate the Parmesan or Pecorino and swirl it though. Continue to simmer if you like your soup thicker.

Ladle into bowls and top with asparagus tips and Parmesan or Pecorino shavings.

**Prep time:**
25 minutes

**Cooking time:**
45 minutes

**Serves 4–6**

# CARROT SOUP WITH ORANGE AND STAR ANISE

One of the very first soups we served in the Pantry was a classic carrot with coriander, and in the couple of years since, we've come up with lots of variations for our members to try. This is a recent discovery: the zingy orange really perks up the flavour, and the star anise adds a hint of warm spices. A great way to rescue a common surplus vegetable from going limp in your fridge.

## INGREDIENTS

**2** onions

**3** garlic cloves

**12** sprigs of thyme

**800g** carrots

**1 tsp** coriander seeds

**1** orange

**2 tbsp** olive oil

**1** star anise

**1.5 litres** vegetable stock

**1 tsp** white wine vinegar

**1 tbsp** butter (optional)

Salt and pepper

## METHOD

Peel and finely chop the onions and garlic. Strip the thyme leaves from the stalks (save the stalks to infuse in vinegar for salad dressings). Peel and cut the carrots into 2cm dice. Crush the coriander seeds in the pestle and mortar until finely ground. Juice the orange.

Set a large saucepan or shallow casserole pan on a medium heat. Add the oil followed by the onions, garlic, star anise, and freshly ground coriander. Gently sauté until all the veg is soft and tender, about 5 minutes.

Add the carrot and thyme leaves. Cook on a low heat for 10 minutes until the carrots are just starting to caramelise. Pour in the stock – the liquid should just cover the vegetables but top up with more stock if required. Bring to the boil, then simmer on a low heat for around 30 minutes.

When the carrots are tender, remove the star anise and blend until the soup is very smooth. Add salt, pepper, and white wine vinegar to taste. Slowly add the orange juice: add half first as you blend, then taste and add more as needed.

If using butter, whisk into the hot soup right before serving (it adds a lovely creamy finish) and serve immediately. Serve hot, garnished with herbs and a drizzle of olive oil.

### NO STRESS BREAD
Our challah rolls go beautifully with this soup.

# CELERIAC, KALE, APPLE, AND CHILLI SOUP

*Donated by Restaurant Associates*

We first met the Restaurant Associates team in 2022 and are delighted to have them as a culinary partner. They are generous about sharing their incredible chefs with us, including Dan Batten, who has taught many of our residents essential cooking skills. Most recently, he mentored our second Community Brigade through training and into employment. Ben Tamlyn, who donated this recipe, describes this soup as "a celebration of seasonal produce and comforting flavours."

## INGREDIENTS

**1** celeriac

**200g** kale

**2** apples

**1–2** red chillies
(more or less to taste)

**1** onion

**2** garlic cloves

**2 tbsp** olive oil

**1.5 litres** vegetable or chicken stock

Salt and pepper

### GARNISH

A handful of fresh herbs
(chives or parsley)

Slices of fresh chilli

## METHOD

Peel the celeriac and cut into 2cm pieces. Strip the kale leaves from the woody stalks (save the stalks for another use – they're great pickled) and finely chop the leaves. Peel, core, and cut the apples into 2cm pieces. Finely chop the chillies (halve and deseed first, for milder heat). Peel and finely chop the onion and garlic.

Set a large saucepan or shallow casserole pan on a medium heat. Add the olive oil, chopped onion, and garlic. Sauté until soft and translucent, about 5 minutes.

Add the celeriac, kale, and apple to the pan and stir to combine with the onion and garlic. Pour in the stock, ensuring that the vegetables are fully submerged, and bring the broth to a gentle simmer. Allow to simmer for 20–25 minutes or until the celeriac is tender and easily pierced with a fork.

Once the vegetables are cooked, blend the soup until smooth. Season the soup with salt and pepper to taste and stir in the chopped red chillies for a hint of heat.

Ladle the broth into bowls and garnish with a sprinkle of fresh herbs, a drizzle of olive oil, and chilli slices, if desired.

# ALEC EROTOKRITOU

Alec Erotokritou has had quite a life. Opening his phone, the dapper 85-year-old shows a photograph of him as a boy standing, tanned and serious, next to the King of Greece. Born in Egypt into a family with little money, when he was 16 he was chosen, against the odds, to travel to Greece as part of an international scouting group and received a trophy from the King. He got to go on adventures he could have never dreamed of, while raising money for people in need.

During the Second World War, he moved to Cyprus, where his father served in the Allied Forces. After the war, barely an adult, Alec worked for the Ministry of Agriculture and set up a small farm. But he wanted a new adventure and as soon as he could get a passport on his 21st birthday, he moved to the UK.

"I arrived in London in 1963, with just a bag," he says with a smile. He went on to start several dressmaking companies while also raising money for charities, including a school for children with additional needs. "It was very hard work, but lots of fun – I don't know how to stop!"

That remains evident even in his advanced years. He explains that since retiring he has been determined to stay active and healthy ("If you are in your chair with a blanket and a mug of cocoa, it's not going to help your body with your arthritis and diabetes"). Still living with the after effects of prostate cancer, Alec insists that he doesn't want anyone to feel sorry for him.

When he started coming to Cook for Good, he was soon "hooked." "It was so different from other community centres I went to," he says. "I kept on going with friends to other places, but the moment I came to this one, it was like an explosion; it was special. And then some of my friends also started coming. We all find it so pleasurable being here, not only for food but for all the rest of the activities they do."

Alec says it is the relentless optimism and the sense that anything is possible at Cook for Good that he really appreciates. The team is always thinking of new ways to help, new courses they can run, or different experts they can invite to meet members. There is a sense of forward momentum that chimes with his own outlook on life.

"The other places are trying their best, but these are difficult times, and good luck to them," he says. "But here, instead of looking backward and accepting reality, they keep on moving forward to make people happier, more comfortable, and more able to do things they couldn't do in the past."

Since becoming a member, Alec has taken part in the Men's Grub Club, enjoys coming to the community meals, and is a regular at the Thursday Pantry. A social butterfly, he enjoys the opportunity to cook, share a meal, and chat.

"After we have finished cooking at Grub Club, we switch plates, and you take and taste what you want," he says. "We sit, we enjoy… and if there is anything extra, we take it home!"

But Alec also wants to help and give back; he understands that he has plenty to offer the organisation and that the relationship between members and organisers is fluid. So, he organises boat trips for older members or encourages others to come to the theatre with secret cheap tickets that he and his friends snap up.

"We like this place so much that we've offered to see what we can do to help," he says. "There are sometimes ideas at other clubs that might work here. So, we are trying to do what we can, and we're not doing badly so far."

Alec talks about the help and support that Cook for Good gives local pensioners, many of whom would otherwise be isolated or struggle to make ends meet. "The Pantry really makes the pennies go a bit further for pensioners," he says. "They are also looking after our health, making sure we can use simple ingredients and start cooking for ourselves a little bit more, and it's healthier at the same time."

Reflecting on what Cook for Good has given him, he says: "It gives me a sense of anticipation. I look forward to coming here and meeting up with everyone. It's now a must in my life – a big, big must. I will never want to stop coming here, unless I die, of course, and then maybe I will still try!"

*Interview by Alexandra Topping*

**Prep time:**
45 minutes

**Cooking time:**
40 minutes

**Serves 4–6**

## INGREDIENTS

**7** red peppers

**4 tbsp** olive oil

**350g** shallots

**1** small bulb fennel

**7** garlic cloves

**1 litre** vegetable stock

Salt and pepper

### WILD GARLIC PESTO

**50g** wild garlic

**50g** basil

**2 tbsp** pine nuts

**20g** Parmesan or Pecorino cheese

**1** garlic clove

**180ml** olive oil

Salt and pepper

### GARNISH

**4–6** slices of ciabatta or bread of your choice

**40–60g** cream cheese

**20–30g** wild garlic pesto or pesto of your choice

Fresh dill

A drizzle of olive oil

# ROASTED RED PEPPER AND FENNEL SOUP WITH WILD GARLIC PESTO

*Donated by Genuine Dining*

Genuine Dining have been great friends to us from our earliest days and continue to support us as culinary partners, including helping us to develop microenterprise projects and offering work experience to our Community Brigades. This simple but delicious recipe has been donated by their chef Mircel McSween, who taught our first Community Brigade. The pesto is a glorious addition that is well worth your time.

## METHOD

Preheat the oven to 180°C/Gas mark 4.

Quarter the red peppers. Cut out the stalks and scoop out the seeds. Cut into chunks and arrange on a roasting tray. Drizzle with 2 tablespoons of the olive oil and season with salt and pepper. Roast in the oven for 20 minutes or until soft and slightly charred.

While the peppers are roasting, finely dice the shallots and fennel. Peel and finely chop the garlic. Set a large saucepan or a shallow casserole pan over a medium heat. Add the remaining 2 tablespoons of olive oil along with the shallot, fennel, and garlic. Sauté until tender but not coloured, around 5–10 minutes.

Add the stock and the roasted peppers. Cover the pan with a lid and leave to simmer for 10 minutes. Then, blend until smooth and keep warm until ready to serve.

To make the pesto, roughly chop the basil and leaves from the wild garlic (if not using wild garlic then just replace with extra basil). Lightly toast the pine nuts in a dry frying pan. Finely grate the Parmesan. Blend the olive oil, garlic clove, toasted pine nuts, Parmesan, along with the wild garlic and basil until you have reached a coarse consistency (not too smooth and not too chunky). Season to taste and spoon into a bowl.

To finish the soup, lightly toast the ciabatta and spread with cream cheese followed by the pesto. Serve the soup warm and garnish with olive oil and fresh dill along with the cream cheese and pesto ciabatta.

**Prep time:**
15 minutes

**Cooking time:**
40 minutes

**Serves 4–6**

# FENNEL AND POTATO SOUP

Our favourite 'accidental' soup, this was created by one of our chefs when we had a surplus of fennel delivered to the Pantry which no one wanted to take because they weren't sure how to use it. It's a twist on the traditional leek and potato soup, so you can swap the leeks back in or use a blend of the two, but we actually prefer this recipe. It certainly convinced our fennel sceptics to start taking it home.

## INGREDIENTS

**1** onion

**2** garlic cloves

**4** medium floury potatoes

**2–3** bulbs of fennel

**3 tbsp** olive oil or butter

**½ tsp** caraway seeds
(option for extra aniseed flavour)

**1.5 litres** vegetable stock

Salt and pepper

## METHOD

Peel and finely chop the onions and garlic. Peel and cut the potatoes into 2cm pieces. Finely chop the fennel – you can save the fennel tops for garnish or add to the soup, as desired.

Set a large saucepan or shallow casserole pan on a medium heat. Add the olive oil or butter followed by the onion and garlic and a good pinch of salt. Stir well and cook for around 7 minutes on a low heat until the onions are tender. Add the fennel and cook for a further 3 minutes. Then add the potatoes, caraway seeds, and vegetable stock. Bring to the boil, then lower the heat and simmer for 15 minutes or until the vegetables are soft.

Blend the soup until silky smooth, adding a little more vegetable stock if it feels too thick. Return the soup to the pan and season to taste.

**TOP IT OFF**     Finish the soup with a drizzle of cream, snipped chives, or fennel tops. It's also lovely with our garlic and herb croutons.

❝ The Pantry has had a very positive impact on my diet, as well as how to feed my family. It also makes me feel like I am part of something greater. ❞

*Pantry member*

# A MEAL IN A BOWL

We like soup so much we could eat it all day long – but if it's your main meal, it's always worth erring on the side of hearty. Whether you throw in some meat or fish or add handfuls of noodles, pulses, or pasta, a chunky soup is a fabulously filling meal that doesn't need anything on the side (and tends to be light on washing up too). Here are some much loved recipes from us and the wider CFG family.

**Prep time:**
15 minutes, plus 30 minutes soaking

**Cooking time:**
1 hour 15 minutes, plus 1 hour cooling time for the stock

**Serves 4–6**

## INGREDIENTS

**85g** dried green lentils

**1** onion

**2** garlic cloves

**1** large carrot

**2** celery sticks

**6** ripe tomatoes

**1** large courgette

**50g** cavolo nero

**30g** parsley

**2 tbsp** olive oil

**½ tsp** cumin seeds

**½ tsp** fennel seeds

**1 tsp** ras al hanout

**4** sprigs of thyme

**1 × 400g** tin chickpeas

**1.5–2 litres** vegetable stock

Salt and pepper

### SEEDED GARNISH

**4 tbsp** reserved chickpeas

**1 tbsp** vegetable oil

**2 tbsp** cashews

**2 tbsp** sunflower seeds

**1 tbsp** pine nuts

**1 tsp** sesame seeds

**2** sprigs of thyme

Zest of **1** lemon

**10g** parsley

# FRAGRANT CHICKPEA SOUP WITH SEEDED GARNISH

*Donated by BaxterStorey*

BaxterStorey is one of our culinary partners, supporting us in a number of ways, including lending us chefs to run children's cooking classes and hosting chef days in our kitchen. This recipe has been donated by Andy Aston, who loves soup as much as we do and is a frequent visiting chef at Cook for Good. He says, "There is nothing more warming or reassuring than a bowl of delicious comforting soup," and this hearty chickpea bowl is a perfect example.

## METHOD

Soak the lentils for 30 minutes in cold water. Drain and rinse well. Peel and finely chop the onion. Peel and thinly slice the garlic. Peel and cut the carrot into 1cm dice. Trim and cut the celery into 1cm dice. Cut the tomatoes into 1cm dice. Trim the courgette and cut into 1cm dice. Wash the cavolo nero, remove and discard the central stalk, and roughly chop the leaves. Finely chop the parsley.

Set a large saucepan or shallow casserole pan over a medium heat. Add the olive oil followed by the onion, garlic, carrot, celery, and a little salt. Cook and stir until softened. Add the cumin seeds, fennel seeds, ras al hanout, and lentils. Strip the thyme leaves from the stalks; discard the stalks, add the leaves and 1.5 litres of stock. Cook over a gentle heat for 20 minutes.

Drain and rinse the chickpeas, saving 4 tbsp for the garnish. Then add the chickpeas (minus the garnish), tomatoes, courgettes, and more stock if needed. Cook for a further 10 minutes, then stir in the cavolo nero and parsley. Season with salt and pepper.

For the garnish, set a frying pan over a medium heat. Add the chickpeas and oil. Toast for a moment. Roughly chop the cashews and add with the sunflower seeds and pine nuts. Lightly toast. Add the sesame seeds, thyme, and lemon zest. Take off the heat. Stir in the parsley. Season, to taste.

To serve, spoon the soup into bowls and finish with the garnish.

## INGREDIENTS

**1** onion

**3** garlic cloves

**1** large carrot

**1** medium potato

**1** lemon

**25g** parsley

**2 tbsp** olive oil

**3 tbsp** tomato puree

**1 tsp** cumin

**1 tsp** pul biber

**½ tsp** dried oregano

**½ tsp** freshly ground black pepper

**½ tsp** cayenne (optional)

**1.5 litres** vegetable stock

**240g** red lentils

**1½ tsp** dried mint

Salt and pepper

### PUL BIBER OIL

**40ml** vegetable oil

**1 tsp** pul biber

# AYSE AND SUE'S TURKISH RED LENTIL SOUP (MERCIMEK CORBASI)

Ayse and her mum, Sue, have been part of the Cook for Good family since our earliest days: Ayse was one of our first volunteers, and Sue is now on our staff team. They told us all about this traditional Turkish soup, so we tried our best to recreate it for Ayse's birthday, presenting it to her (slightly nervously) instead of a cake. You can imagine how delighted we were when Ayse told us it was just like her Nene used to make.

## METHOD

Peel and finely chop the onion and garlic. Peel and cut the carrot and potato into 2cm dice. Cut the lemon into 6 wedges. Finely chop the parsley.

Set a large saucepan or shallow casserole pan over a medium heat. Add the olive oil followed by the onion and sauté for 5 minutes or until translucent. Add the diced carrot and potato and sauté again, stirring occasionally, for a further 5 minutes. Add the garlic and cook, stirring, for about 30 seconds (don't burn).

Add the tomato puree, cumin, pul biber, oregano, a good pinch of salt, black pepper, and cayenne, if using. Stir for 30 seconds and then deglaze the bottom of the pan with a small amount of water. Add the stock and lentils. Stir and increase the heat until the soup is boiling. Reduce the heat and allow to simmer for 20–25 minutes, stirring occasionally, until the vegetables are tender and the lentils are cooked through. If the soup is getting too thick, add a little water.

Remove the soup from the heat and stir in the dried mint and a squeeze of juice from one of the lemon wedges. Now you can leave as is or use a stick blender to blend the soup until it's creamy and all the ingredients are incorporated.

To make the pul biber oil, just heat the oil in a small pan and add the pul biber. Stir to combine and remove from heat. Continue to stir until fully incorporated.

Serve the soup with the remaining lemon wedges, a sprinkle of chopped parsley, and a drizzle of the pul biber oil.

## INGREDIENTS

**1** medium butternut squash

**1** red pepper

**1** onion

**1** garlic clove

A small thumb of ginger (approx. **5cm**)

**1** dried red chilli

**1 tbsp** vegetable oil

**1 tbsp** coconut oil or ghee

**1** stick cinnamon

**1 tsp** Jaffna or roasted Sri Lankan curry powder (or Madras curry powder)

**8–10** curry leaves

**850ml** vegetable or chicken stock

**2 tbsp** double cream (optional)

Salt and pepper

### TOP IT OFF
Elevate this amazing soup even further with a dollop of crème fraiche. Finish with a sprinkle of toasted pumpkin and sunflower seeds.

### NO STRESS BREAD
We love it paired it with Amel's matlou-a.

# KARAN GOKANI'S SRI LANKAN CURRIED BUTTERNUT SQUASH SOUP

Karan's Hoppers restaurant is based near Kings Cross, and when we cheekily asked him at our first meeting if he'd be willing to get involved, he replied, "Whatever you need." He also created a banana leaf feast for our second fundraising Supper Club, donating the food as well as his and his chefs' time. We all love this recipe, which he describes as: "An easy weeknight supper, when you're craving something spicy and adventurous but still want the comfort of a quick meal."

## METHOD

Preheat the oven to 200°C/Gas mark 6.

Peel, deseed, and cut the butternut squash into 2cm cubes. Deseed the red pepper and chop into 2cm cubes. Peel and thinly slice the onion. Peel and finely chop the garlic. Peel and finely grate the ginger. Deseed the dried chilli.

Drizzle the vegetable oil and a generous pinch of salt over the squash and roast it in a preheated oven for 20 minutes or until slightly coloured and cooked through.

Set a large saucepan or shallow casserole pan over a medium heat. Add the coconut oil or ghee. Once melted, add the cinnamon stick, garlic, ginger, and onion.

After a couple of minutes, add the dried chilli, curry powder, curry leaves, and red pepper. Fry for a further 2 minutes. Then add the squash and stock, give it all a good mix, and simmer for 15 minutes.

Fish out the cinnamon stick and blend until you have a smooth texture, adding some water or more stock, if required, to reach the consistency of soup you like.

Bring the soup back to a gentle simmer, stir in the cream (if using) and season to taste. Karan recommends a good hit (about ½ tsp) of coarsely ground black peppercorns for depth of flavour and gentle heat.

# IRMA'S MINESTRONE

**Prep time:**
30 minutes

**Cooking time:**
1 hour

**Serves 4–6**

This is the soup that Robinne grew up on. Her mum, Irma, used to make it on a wet and windy day, and although Irma passed away in 2020, her recipe lives on in the Pantry. It was one of the first soups we made for a community cooking demo, and it's been regularly enjoyed by our members ever since. They tell us they love to add a bit of pesto to make it extra Italian. We think Irma would have been happy with that.

## INGREDIENTS

**1** onion

**1** large carrot

**1** celery stick

**125g** white cabbage

**75g** spinach

**1** small courgette

**2 × 400g** tins chopped tomatoes

**2** bay leaves

**1 tsp** dried oregano

**2.5 litres** vegetable stock

**100g** macaroni or soup pasta

**1 ×** small tin cannellini beans
(**120g** drained weight)

**150g** sweetcorn kernels
(frozen or drained tinned)

**50g** Parmesan or Pecorino cheese

**25g** parsley

Salt and pepper

## METHOD

Peel and finely dice the onion. Peel the carrot and cut into 1cm dice. Cut the celery and courgette into 1cm dice. Thinly slice the cabbage. Add all the veg to a large saucepan or a shallow casserole pan.

Add the tinned tomatoes, bay leaf, and oregano. Season well with salt and pepper. Add enough stock (about 2 litres) to cover all the veg and add a bit extra. Mix everything together well and cover. Bring to the boil, then turn down to a simmer and cook until the vegetables are tender, about 30 minutes.

When the veg is soft, add the pasta and more stock if required (about 500ml). Cook for a further 15 minutes until the pasta is soft.

While the soup is cooking, wash the spinach – roughly chop if using large leaves but leave baby leaves whole. Drain the beans. Finely grate the cheese. Finely chop the parsley. When the soup is cooked, turn off the heat and add the beans, sweetcorn, spinach, and parsley. Mix well. Check seasoning and add salt and pepper to taste.

Leave the soup off the heat for the flavours to infuse and serve with the grated cheese.

# ESIN OZEN

Esin Ozen is the first to admit that she didn't used to think too much about other people's hardships. She moved to the UK from Turkey when she was 26 and threw herself into her new life. She started working as a kitchen and bar manager in a pub, working long hours, and having a lot of fun.

"I was in my 20s, and I was just really enjoying myself. I was healthy, active, and I just worked like crazy," she reminisces. She met her now ex-husband and got pregnant – and then everything changed.

They separated and divorced when she was in the early stages of pregnancy, and she brought her baby into the world as a single parent. It soon became clear that her son, now six, had additional needs. "As a mother you don't really know what to do, so you read more, and you cry more, and you try to find help."

When the pandemic hit, she became desperate, feeling that there was no chance of getting the diagnosis and help her toddler needed. She escaped to Turkey and found intensive therapy for her son, but when the pubs opened and then shut again, she had to return to work.

"I had to work full time because I had to support us both. I wasn't getting any money from anywhere else, and until he was diagnosed, I was paying for everything privately. It was a really difficult time."

Finally, her son was diagnosed as having autism and ADHD, and Esin thought that there might be a little respite from her worries. But then, two months later, she was diagnosed with multiple sclerosis.

"Then everything just kind of fell apart," she says. "I was extremely independent, but my life completely changed. I could barely walk and mentally – I was gone." Having felt free and fearless for all her youth, she was suddenly desperately vulnerable. "I couldn't talk to anyone about it for quite a long time," she says. "I was scared of people seeing me in a different way. I was scared to show how I was feeling."

She moved to Islington in north London to be closer to her hospital and started getting support from an "amazing" local charity called Brightstar. "I was very lucky because there was one lady there, Dan, who could see that in my heart I wasn't well," she says. "I was focused on looking after my son and making sure he was ok, but she suggested that I try talking to people. But I said I didn't want to talk, I didn't want to listen, I wasn't ready."

But when the woman from Brightstar handed her a leaflet for Cook for Good, it made her reconsider. "I have always loved being in the kitchen, cooking with my glass of wine – it was one of the things that always made me happy, so I thought I would give it a try."

When she walked through the door for the first time, she was met, she says, with an empathy and understanding that had been missing from her life. "Until then, the people I met would say they were listening, but they were not really listening. Everyone said they understood, but they had no idea. Here they really do listen, they really do understand. I used to come feeling heavy, but when I walked through the doors of Cook for Good, I felt like someone actually cared."

Community Manager Martha insisted that Esin give her personal number to the hospital in case of emergencies. "It's like a second home here," she says. "I get all the support I need."

Her experience has completely changed her outlook on life, she explains. "Before I got sick, I never listened to anyone. I was getting on with my life, I was extremely busy – I'm not going to lie," she admits. "But when I came here, I found there were other people who were also going through difficult things and there was something missing in our lives – but here we were filled up."

Cook for Good manages to help people without making them feel embarrassed, she says. "It's not a food bank here; it's like a social market. And you can see there are people who have never been in a coffee shop, but here they can have a nice coffee and maybe some soup and a conversation – they can have that lovely experience."

Now she feels more able to face the challenges in her life: she can talk freely; she can share the burden. She can also help others going through difficult times and has started working as a volunteer. "Cook for Good helps everyone, but I honestly think they have helped me the most," she asserts. "It's given me back my confidence and allowed me to plan for the future. It's helped me to find myself again."

*Interview by Alexandra Topping*

# FISH PIE SOUP

There are few things more comforting than a homemade fish pie, and this simple fish chowder works a similar magic. It's the perfect mid-week meal in a bowl (although guests would love it too!), and it's as versatile as it is satisfying. If you prefer no shellfish then just use an additional 350g of fish pie mix.

## INGREDIENTS

**1** large onion

**225g** new potatoes

**25g** flat-leaf parsley

**1½ tbsp** olive oil

**50g** butter

**1 tbsp** plain white flour

**650ml** fish stock

Pinch of grated nutmeg

Pinch of cayenne

**300ml** milk

**350g** fish pie mix (any mix of smoked/unsmoked fish)

**4 tbsp** single cream

**350g** cooked mixed shellfish

**100g** fresh or frozen peas

Salt and pepper

## METHOD

Peel and finely dice the onion. Dice the new potatoes into 2.5cm cubes. Chop the parsley.

Set a saucepan over a medium heat. Add the olive oil, butter, and onion. Cook for around 10 minutes until the onion is soft. Stir in the flour and cook for another 2 minutes.

Pour in the fish stock and bring to the boil. Add the potatoes, cover, and simmer for 12–15 minutes until the potatoes are cooked through. Add the nutmeg and cayenne and season generously with salt and pepper. Stir in the milk.

Stir in the fish. Simmer for 4 minutes. Add the cream, shellfish, and peas. Simmer a further 3–4 minutes. Add salt and pepper to taste. Serve sprinkled with chopped parsley.

# ED BALLS' PRAWN PHO

Former politician Ed is a seasoned foodie and winner of Celebrity Best Home Cook, who has supported us since our earliest days. He hosted the first ever Cook for Good Supper Club in September 2022, working with our volunteers to cook a three-course meal and demonstrating his signature soufflé for our guests. He fell in love with Vietnamese cooking when he was on Strictly, and while he doesn't always find it easy to get the same light spicy and salty tastes at home, this one really works: "A healthy, fiery soup with a wonderful aroma and deep flavours."

## INGREDIENTS

**3** garlic cloves

**3** lemongrass stalks

**3** red bird's eye chillies

A small thumb of ginger (approx. **5cm**)

A handful fresh coriander leaves

A handful of mint leaves

**1 litre** chicken or vegetable stock

**100g** beansprouts

**100g** vermicelli rice noodles

**400g** peeled tiger prawns

**4 tbsp** fish sauce

**3** limes, quartered

## METHOD

Peel and thinly slice the garlic. Remove the outer layer from the lemongrass stalks, bash with a saucepan to soften, and then cut in half. Finely chop one of the chillies. Bash the ginger with a saucepan to soften. Strip the coriander and mint leaves from the stalks and discard the stalks, reserving the leaves.

Put the stock in a large, heavy-based saucepan. Add the garlic, lemongrass, whole chillies, half of the chopped chilli, and the ginger. Bring to the boil and simmer for 30 minutes. Meanwhile, put the noodles into a saucepan, cover in boiling water, and cook for 4 minutes. Turn off the heat.

Add the prawns and 3 tablespoons of the fish sauce to the stock and simmer for a further 5 minutes. Turn off the heat. Remove the lemongrass, ginger, and whole chillies. Add the beansprouts and a handful each of coriander and mint leaves. Taste for balance and adjust with more fish sauce to taste.

Drain the noodles and place in serving bowls. Ladle over the soup and sprinkle the remaining chopped chilli, mint, and coriander. Serve with the lime quarters on the side.

# CALLALOO SOUP

**Prep time:**
10 minutes

**Cooking time:**
25 minutes

**Serves 4–6**

A traditional Caribbean crab soup, Callaloo is named after the green vegetable whose leaves are used as its base. You can buy tinned callaloo in big supermarkets and online, and if you're lucky enough to have a Caribbean shop in your area, you can probably find it fresh. But if you're struggling to get hold of it, just use spinach instead. The magic of this recipe not only comes from the dark leafy green goodness but also from the depth of flavour created by the pairing of fresh crab and salty bacon.

## INGREDIENTS

**500g** callaloo leaves or spinach

**6** slices lean bacon

**1.25 litres** chicken stock

**1** onion

**1** garlic clove

**3** spring onions

**8** fresh okra

**1** green pepper

**¼ tsp** dried thyme

**225g** crab meat

**1 tbsp** butter

Salt and pepper

## METHOD

Wash and roughly chop the callaloo or spinach leaves. Cut the bacon into 1cm pieces. Peel and finely chop the onion and garlic. Trim and thinly slice the spring onions. Slice the okra in 3mm thick slices. Deseed and cut the green pepper into thin slices.

Put the green leaves, bacon, onion, garlic, spring onions, and thyme in a large saucepan or shallow casserole pan. Pour the stock over and set on a medium heat. Cook for 5–10 minutes until the bacon is cooked through and the vegetables are starting to soften.

Add the crab meat and okra slices and cook for another 15 minutes until the okra is tender. Stir in the butter and season to taste with salt and pepper.

Garnish with the fresh green pepper slices.

## INGREDIENTS

| | |
|---|---|
| **18** tiger prawns | **8** red bird eye chillies |
| **9** button mushrooms | **120ml** fish sauce |
| **6cm** galangal | **1 tbsp** caster sugar |
| **3** lemongrass stalks | **90g** chilli paste in oil |
| **3** banana shallots | **30g** oil from the chilli paste |
| **2** limes | **14** cherry tomatoes |
| **1.5 litre** chicken or vegetable stock | **120ml** coconut milk |
| **9** Kaffir lime leaves | **6** sprigs of coriander |

# WICHET KHONGPHOON'S TOM YUM SOUP

Wichet hosted the third Cook for Good Supper Club in September 2023. His love of tom yum soup began when he worked in Phuket. He says: "It arrived in a big metal bowl with flaming charcoal underneath... there was something special about eating tom yum with my friends by the sea." Zingy, salty, and fragrant with fresh herbs, it's a real favourite at Supawan, Wichet's restaurant, which is just round the corner from Priory Green (and loved by foodies including Nigella and Jay Rayner).

## METHOD

Clean the prawns with cold running water, remove the heads and shells and keep them to make a stock. Keep the tails on for the aesthetic. To remove the prawn's vein, make a shallow cut along the back of the prawn and then remove the black vein. Wash the prawns in cold water.

Clean the mushrooms and cut into quarters. Slice the galangal into 6 pieces. Remove the outer woody layer from the lemongrass and cut each stalk into 3 pieces. Peel the shallots and cut in half lengthways. Juice the limes to yield 120 ml juice.

Next, make the prawn stock. Set a large saucepan or shallow casserole pan on a medium heat. Add all the prawn heads and shells into the dry pan and keep stirring them until the colour of the shell turns pink. Then add 800 ml of the stock, bring to the boil, and simmer for 5 minutes. Add in the rest of the stock. Strain the prawn stock and push down on the shells to get as much flavour and goodness out of them as possible. Discard the heads and shells.

Return the strained stock to your saucepan or casserole pan, and bring to the boil over a medium high heat. Add the chillies (left whole), galangal, lemongrass, shallots, and lime leaves. Then add fish sauce, sugar, and chilli paste and boil for 5 minutes.

Add the whole cherry tomatoes and quartered mushrooms followed by the prawns. Cook the soup for another 2 minutes until the prawns are cooked (they will turn pink). To finish the soup, add half of the coconut milk and lime juice. Tasting the soup, it should be fragrant, sour, spicy, salty, and sweet. Add more lime juice, sugar, coconut milk, or fish sauce to taste.

To serve, spoon the soup into bowls and drizzle some chilli oil and coconut milk on top. Strip the coriander leaves from the stalks and use the leaves to garnish.

**Prep time:**
35 minutes

**Cooking time:**
50 minutes

**Serves 4–6**

# ITALIAN MEATBALL, GNOCCHI, AND KALE SOUP

There's something incredibly therapeutic about making meatball soup. It may not be the speediest process, but it's very relaxing and perfect for the kind of day when you want to stay close to home. Just pop on a podcast or your favourite playlist and indulge in a bit of food-based mindfulness, with the bonus of a hearty meal when you're done. Comfort food from comforting cooking.

## INGREDIENTS

**25g** Parmesan or Pecorino cheese

**15g** parsley

**500g** beef mince (**10%** fat)

**50g** breadcrumbs

**1** large egg

**¾ tsp** dried basil

**¾ tsp** onion powder

**1** large onion

**3** garlic cloves

**3** carrots

**2 tbsp** olive oil

**1.25 litres** chicken stock

**160g** kale

**400g** fresh gnocchi

Salt and pepper

## METHOD

Preheat your oven to 180°C/Gas mark 4.

Finely grate the cheese. Line a baking tray with non-stick baking paper.

Place the beef mince, breadcrumbs, egg, grated cheese, basil, and onion powder in a large bowl with a good pinch of salt and pepper. Mix well to combine everything. Form the mix into small meatballs (about 2cm each in diameter), placing them on the lined baking tray and in the fridge for 15 minutes while you prep the veg.

Peel and finely dice the onion and garlic. Peel and cut the carrots into 2cm dice. Strip the leaves from the kale. Roughly chop the leaves and finely chop the stalks, discarding any tough, woody stalks. Finely chop the parsley.

Roast the meatballs in the preheated oven for 15–20 minutes until coloured.

While the meatballs cook, place a large saucepan on a medium-high heat, add the olive oil followed by the onion and carrot. Sauté until they begin to caramelise, stirring often. Once the meatballs are cooked, add them to the vegetables and pour in the stock.

Add the kale. Season with salt and pepper to taste. Cover the pan and cook for 15 minutes. Stir in the gnocchi and cook for 3 minutes or until tender. Stir through the chopped parsley and serve.

**NO STRESS BREAD**     To make an even heartier meal of it, serve with our green olive and rosemary focaccia.

# RHIZ CHAB

When Rhiz first came to Cook for Good, she felt utterly defeated. She had been suffering domestic abuse for years and feared leaving the house because of her neighbours' anti-social behaviour. But no one had listened.

She just kept putting one foot in front of another, trying to do the best she could for her pre-teen children. She was surviving – just.

"It was a really difficult time," she recalls. "I tried so many different things, knocked on so many different doors, but no one listened to my case."

A friend told her that a new community organisation had started on the Priory Green Estate and invited her along, thinking it might help – it would at least get her out of the house.

Rhiz says that everything changed when she walked through the doors of Cook for Good. She was given training by members of the team and started working as a volunteer. "They gave me training, and then they accepted me, and I started working here. It's beautiful," she says with a small smile, her bangles clinking on her wrist. "I love it. I felt like I was walking into a community."

For the first time since she had arrived in the UK from Morocco for a marriage arranged by her family, someone wanted to hear her story and, finally, someone wanted to help.

"I'm a single mum with three children, and I was homeless. I'm a little bit shy, but when they saw me, they started asking how I was and then what was going on," she says.

Rhiz explains that she had been moved into insecure temporary accommodation, feeling unsafe because her ex-husband knew where she had been placed. She was then moved again to a crumbling hotel on the outskirts of London, where there was no way to heat food and she and her pre-teens were crammed into one room. The hotel was filthy, and the children were bitten by bedbugs.

"The Cook for Good team brought me back," she says. "If it wasn't for them, I would still be there. They made calls, they sent emails. There are no words to describe what they did for me. They stood by my side through everything."

Like many others, Rhiz talks of the staff and members at Cook for Good as a family. "They supported me mentally, physically, and financially as well. They stood behind me and helped me get

strong," she says. "Cook for Good is not just about food, it's not like you buy your food or learn to cook and then go; people stay, we sit and chat, and we share our problems."

Because of the tight-knit nature of the community, everyone looks out for each other, she adds. "People come and sit around the table talking, sharing their feelings and memories. If someone goes missing for a week, they start asking 'what's happened?'"

She says that people who have lived on the estate all their lives sit and share a moment with others, like her, who arrived in the UK more recently. "You can find every nationality here," she says. "French, Spanish, Moroccan, Algerian – everybody has a smile for you, everyone talks, everyone is welcome."

Rhiz explains the huge difference between the organisation's weekly surplus food pantry, where members pay £3.50 each week to choose a basket of food worth between £30 and £35, and a food bank. "People don't feel comfortable going to a food bank; the attitude is different, even the body language is different," she says. "Here people don't go away feeling bad; they feel like they're part of something positive."

Rhiz has now been moved outside London but still travels more than an hour every week to volunteer at the Pantry. She has completed hospitality training and works for Cook for Good at events. Thanks to the support and encouragement she has received, she is also starting up her own business making websites.

During Covid, Rhiz organised online classes to help other mums learn cooking and arts and crafts. These were so popular that she got the idea to create a website called Oum Space (mothers' space) for free online classes with her via Zoom, with the hope that mothers with young children can learn a variety of arts and crafts while building friendships and supporting each other along the way. She has put the idea on hold until she and her children are more settled, but she is excited and happy when talking about her future plans.

By coming to Cook for Good, she has not only found friends and support but also a way back to herself. "If you had met me before, I was a very different person," she says. "But now I feel stronger. Life is not going to finish with me crying; I have to fly."

*Interview by Alexandra Topping*

**Prep time:**
20 minutes

**Cooking time:**
2 hr 45 minutes

**Serves 4–6**

# BEEF AND BARLEY SOUP

We often have barley delivered to the Pantry, and when we noticed that it was getting left on the shelves, Robinne cooked up this recipe to show our members how to use it. It's a classic broth, wholesome, warming, and filling enough for your evening meal. Just remember to start making it a good few hours before you want to eat it as the beef needs to simmer to make it tender – it's worth every minute.

## INGREDIENTS

**1** large onion

**2** small or **1** large carrot

**1** celery stick

Half a large or **1** small leek

**1** medium potato

**100g** swede

**2 tbsp** olive oil

**1** thick slice beef shin (bone in)

**100g** mixed or spring greens

**1.5 litres** vegetable or beef stock

**3 tbsp** tomato puree

**2** bay leaves

**100g** pearl barley

Salt and pepper

## METHOD

Peel and finely chop the onion. Peel and cut the carrot into 1cm dice. Cut the celery into 1cm dice. Thinly slice the leek, ensuring it's really clean first. Peel and cut the potato and swede into 1–2cm dice.

Set a large saucepan or shallow casserole pan on a medium-high heat. Add the oil followed by the beef. Season with salt and pepper. Sear on both sides until lightly caramelised. Remove. Set aside.

Return the pan to the heat. Add the diced onion, carrot, and celery. Cook for 5 minutes or until tender. Add the leek and more oil, if needed. Lower heat. Sauté until tender. Stir in the potato and swede. Cook a further 5 minutes or until just softened. Wash the mixed greens. Roughly chop any larger leaves; leave baby leaves whole. Fold into the soup.

Reduce the heat to medium. Add the tomato puree and bay leaves. Cook for 1 minute. Add the beef back to the pan followed by the stock, which should cover all the ingredients. Add more stock or top up with water, if needed. Mix well and bring to the boil. Lower the heat, cover, and simmer for 2 hours or until everything is tender.

Cook the barley by bringing a large pan salted of water to the boil, add the barley, then simmer until the barley is tender, about 25 minutes. Drain and rinse. When the veg and meat are soft, remove the meat with a slotted spoon. Partly blend the vegetables to soften the texture while keeping it a bit chunky.

Stir the cooked barley into the soup. If too thick, thin with hot water. Allow the meat to cool slightly and then flake it back into the soup, removing any gristle or bone. Season the soup with salt and pepper to taste. Serve hot.

# NIGELLA'S YELLOW SPLIT PEA AND FRANKFURTER SOUP

Nigella Lawson has been one of our foodie supporters since we first began, and our community loved chatting about food and swapping recipes with her when she popped into the Pantry for a visit. This embracingly hearty recipe is one she has often made for a cosy family New Year's Day lunch: in her words, "When you come back home, hands, nose, and feet stinging from the cold, this is just what you need to have waiting for you."

## INGREDIENTS

**1** onion

**1** carrot

**1** garlic clove

**1** celery stick

**2–3 tbsp** vegetable oil

½ teaspoon ground nutmeg

**500g** yellow split peas

**1.5 litres** vegetable or chicken stock

**2** bay leaves

Approx. **8** frankfurter sausages

## METHOD

Peel the onion, carrot, and garlic. Cut the onion and carrot into rough chunks. Roughly cut up a stick of celery. Put them all, along with the celery, into the bowl of a food processor. Blitz until finely chopped.

Spoon the oil into a heavy-based wide saucepan and put on medium heat. When warm, add the oil, followed by the chopped vegetables from the processor and cook for 5–10 minutes, until soft but not coloured.

Add the ground nutmeg – this may be a small amount but it's crucial to the taste – give a good stir and then add the split peas and stir again until they're glossily mixed with the oil-slicked, cooked-down vegetables. Pour over 1.25 litres stock and add the bay leaves, then bring to the boil. Cover, turn down the heat and cook for about an hour until everything is tender and sludgy, adding more stock as needed. Sometimes the peas seem to thicken too much before they actually cook and need to be watered down. Taste for seasoning once everything's ready.

You can add the frankfurters as you wish. It's probably easiest just to cut them into slices of about 3cm each and throw them into the soup to warm.

# RHIMOU'S FAST-BREAKING LAMB HARIRA SOUP

**Prep time:**
15 minutes,
plus 30 minutes soaking

**Cooking time:**
2 hours

**Serves 4–6**

One of the joys of Cook for Good is getting to talk about food with members of our community from across the world. During our first Ramadan at Priory Green, volunteer Rhimou brought in a pan of this soup and some dates, which she and her family eat to break their fast at the end of a long day. It's one of their favourites, and now it's one of ours too. Packed with protein and delicious flavours, it's the perfect post-sundown meal.

## INGREDIENTS

**70g** dried green lentils

**350g** boneless lamb neck

**1** onion

**2** garlic cloves

**1** carrot

**2** celery sticks

**1 tsp** turmeric

**1 tsp** ground cumin

**½ tsp** ground ginger

**½ tsp** cinnamon

**½ tsp** cayenne pepper

**1 tbsp** vegetable or olive oil

**2 × 400g** tins chopped tomatoes

**1 litre** vegetable stock

**2 tbsp** tomato puree

**1 × 400g** tin chickpeas

**50g** broken vermicelli

**25g** fresh coriander

**25g** parsley

**½** lemon

Salt and pepper

## METHOD

Soak the lentils in cold water. Dice the lamb into small cubes, removing excess fat. Peel and finely chop the onion and garlic. Peel and cut the carrots into 1cm dice. Cut the celery into 1cm dice. Make up the spice mix with all the dry spices.

Set a large saucepan or shallow casserole pan on a medium heat. Once hot, add the oil. Brown the meat well (in batches if necessary) and then remove from the pan. Add the carrot, onion, and celery to the pan with a pinch of salt. Sauté, stirring regularly until softened. Add the garlic and spices and cook for 1–2 minutes, stirring regularly, until the spices are aromatic.

Return the meat to the pan. Season with salt and pepper. Add the tinned tomatoes and stock. Bring to the boil and then turn down the heat, cover, and simmer on a low heat until the meat is soft (around 1 hour).

Drain and rinse the lentils. Add to the pan and cook until soft, around 15–20 minutes. Stir in the tomato puree. Cook for a moment while you drain and rinse the tinned chickpeas. Add the chickpeas and vermicelli. Cook for another 15 minutes or until the vermicelli is just cooked.

Finely chop the coriander and parsley. Take the soup off the heat. Stir in the herbs. Season with salt and pepper to taste. Serve the soup warm, with a good squeeze of lemon juice. If the soup is too thick, you can add a little hot water to loosen.

**NO STRESS BREAD**     Try this soup with our delicious warm flatbreads, which are especially good glossed with butter.

# TOPPING IT OFF

There's nothing like a topping to make a good soup great. It can help bring out subtle flavours, sharpen up the seasoning, deepen the texture, or just add a really satisfying crunch. We like to serve a choice of toppings with our Pantry soups every Thursday, and we've included the ones that get spooned or sprinkled most liberally here. You'll find recommendations for which toppings work best with which soups throughout the book.

## INGREDIENTS

**30g** Parmesan or Pecorino cheese

**1** garlic clove (optional)

**50g** nuts or seeds, alone or in combination (pine nuts, hazelnuts, cashew, walnuts, almonds, macadamia, peanuts, sunflower seeds, pumpkin seeds, sesame seeds, etc.)

**60g** herbs or leaves – a combination of whatever you have left over, including stalks if soft (basil, coriander, spinach, rocket, watercress, etc.)

**100–150ml** olive oil

½ lemon

Salt and pepper

# PESTO

This is our classic pesto and the joy of it is that you can use it as a canvas for all sorts of herbs or green leaves. We have two other brilliant pesto recipes as a key element to two of our soups: one features wild garlic as the dominant green and the other walnuts as a signature nut. Both hint at some of the fun flavour possibilities with which you can tailor the garnish to accentuate the character of your soup. For example, whizz coriander and cashews into a pesto for an Asian-flavoured soup (like our butternut, sweet potato, and coconut soup).

## METHOD

Finely grate the cheese. Peel the garlic clove, if using. Combine the grated cheese and peeled garlic with the nuts or seeds, the herbs or leaves, 100ml of the olive oil, a squeeze of lemon juice, and a good pinch of salt and pepper.

Blend to bring everything together, adding more oil if needed. Taste and add more salt or pepper if needed.

> **"** I didn't know what to with the lentils I had in my cupboard for ages, then I tasted the lentil and tomato soup at the pantry, took the recipe home and made it. I shared it with my family in Nigeria and America and now they make it too. **"**
>
> *Pantry member*

# TOMATO SALSA

**Prep time:**
15 minutes

**Serves 4–6**

## INGREDIENTS

**4** tomatoes

¼ small red onion

**10g** fresh coriander

½ small mild red chilli

½ lime

A pinch of sugar

½ **tsp** white wine vinegar

Salt and pepper

A zingy tomato salsa is a delicious way to add a fresh finish and tangy contrast to soups. It's particularly delicious with our Mexican chicken and black bean soup, adding flavour as well as an additional portion of veg.

## METHOD

Wash the tomatoes, slice into 5mm thick slices, then cut across into strips and then a fine dice. Cut the onion into a very fine dice and add to the tomatoes. Destalk and finely chop the coriander leaves. Mix the coriander through the tomatoes. Deseed and finely dice a mild chilli and add to taste. Squeeze in some lime juice. Season with salt and pepper. Add a pinch of sugar and the vinegar.

Stir and adjust seasoning to taste.

# GREMOLATA

This Italian condiment is like a cross between pesto and salsa. It adds refreshing colour and contrast to rich creamy soups. We love it with our fennel and potato soup. It's a clever condiment too. The vitamin C from the lemon helps you absorb the natural iron from the parsley, and the parsley negates the punchy, breath-affecting notes of the garlic.

## METHOD

Trim away the toughest of the parsley stalks before chopping the rest of the bunch very finely. Peel and grate the garlic and use a fine grater (e.g., a microplane) to grate the zest of the lemons.

Combine all the ingredients on your chopping board and continue to chop until everything is combined and the mix is really fine. You can substitute other herbs or even other citrus fruits for interesting combinations.

**Prep time:**
10 minutes

**Serves 4–6**

## INGREDIENTS

**50g** parsley

**1** garlic clove

**2** lemons

# HERB-INFUSED CREAM

A ripple of cream not only looks a treat in a velvety bowl of soup but also gives an irresistible texture and flavour contrast. Infuse fresh herbs in your cream, and you amplify the results. Try tarragon-infused cream with our cream of mushroom soup or basil-infused cream with the broccoli stalk soup.

## METHOD

Creams can be infused using either the hot or cold method. For the hot method, roughly chop your herbs (or leave whole – best for basil which can bruise and brown easily when chopped) and add to the cream in a medium saucepan. Heat until just boiling, then switch off immediately. Steep the herbs in the cream for 10–20 minutes, checking the intensity after 10 minutes and in 5-minute intervals thereafter.

For the cold method, add the chopped herbs to the cream and place in the fridge for 7 hours or overnight.

After the infusion (hot or cold), strain the cream and discard the herbs. It will last for up to 3 days in the fridge.

**Prep time:**
5 minutes

**Cooking time:**
20 minutes (hot infused),
or 7 hours (cold infused)

**Makes 250ml**

## INGREDIENTS

**200g** soft herbs
(e.g., basil, chives, coriander, parsley, tarragon, wild garlic)

**300ml** double cream

# HERB OILS

Imbuing oil with the scented delights of herbs is a brilliant way to extract a concentration of colour and flavour – and to use up an abundance of herbs. Herb oils are also ideal swaps for ripples of cream for non-dairy diets. Try a chive oil with our green goddess soup (swap with wild garlic when it's in season) or coriander oil with our curried parsnip soup.

**Prep time:**
15 minutes

**Cooking time:**
1 minute

**Makes 200ml**

## INGREDIENTS

**200g** soft herbs (e.g., basil, chives, parsley, coriander)

**300ml** olive oil or groundnut oil

Salt (for the water)

## METHOD

Bring a large saucepan of salted water to the boil. Prepare a large bowl filled with ice and water next to the pan.

Once the water is boiling, add the herbs and blanche for around 30 seconds. Remove from the pan with a slotted spoon and plunge immediately into the iced water to refresh and cool. Once the herbs are completely cold, transfer them to a clean dry tea towel to dry. Get as much moisture as possible out of the herbs.

Transfer the herbs to a food processor and add the oil. Blend until completely smooth. If the mixture feels very thick, you can add more oil. This can take up to 5 minutes at high speed.

Line a sieve with a double layer of muslin or a coffee filter. Pour the oil into the sieve and allow it to seep through slowly into a container. This can be done overnight in the fridge. Once completed, transfer to a clean bottle and store in the fridge for up to two weeks.

## VARIATION

**CHILLI OIL**     For a chilli oil, swap the herbs for 3 dried chillies. Gently warm the oil in a saucepan with the chillies and simmer for 5 minutes. Take off the heat. Allow to cool fully, then transfer into a bottle with the chillies. Leave to continue infusing in the bottle. Store in the fridge for up to 1 month.

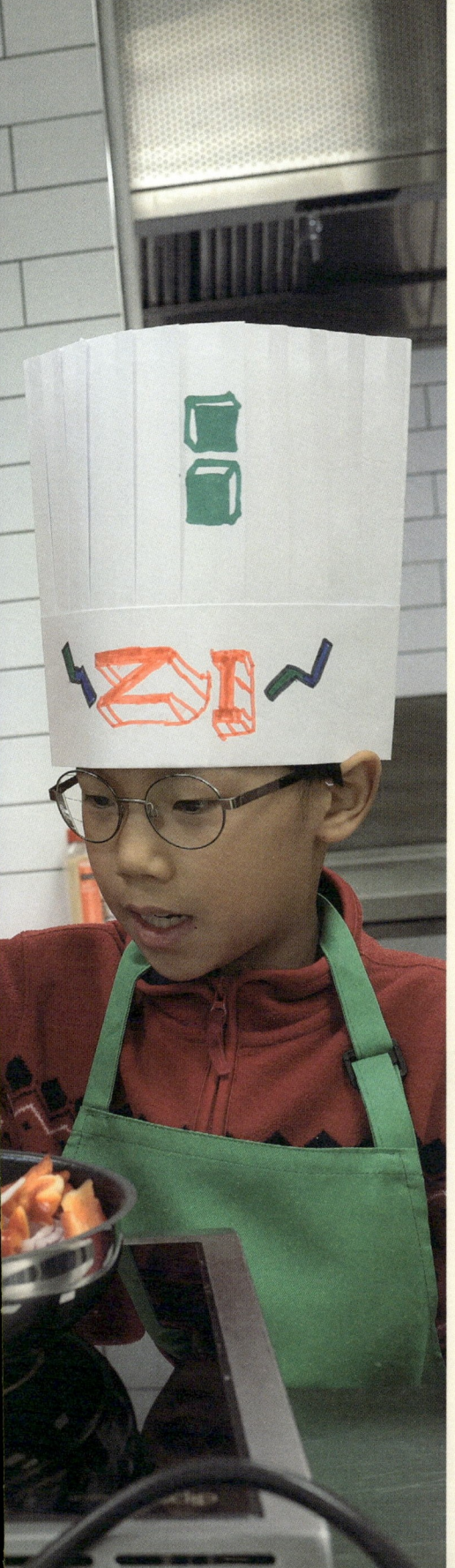

# WILLIAM LAU

William Lau doesn't have fond memories of being in the kitchen. He explains that he and his sister worked in his family's take-away, alongside their parents who both came to the UK from Hong Kong with little money. He recalls that they worked after school, at weekends, and during the holidays when they were at university.

So, when he came to the professional kitchen at Cook for Good for a cookery class with his two children, he was hit by a deluge of memories. "It's quite a common thing for British-born Chinese kids to be put to work," he says. "When I came into this commercial-grade kitchen, it actually reminded me a bit of working in the takeaway. We were making quesadillas and the kids had to peel an onion, and I remembered that my sister and I each had to peel a sack of onions, which was 18 kilos."

Instead of being a stressful environment fraught with colourful language, he found the Cook for Good kitchen full of kindness and laughter. "Our kids don't have to be in a kitchen because they have no choice," he says. "They are there for fun; they are enjoying it. It's a little bit less stressful than the lives my sister and I led."

William is a teacher now, based at Great Ormond Street Hospital where he teaches computer science at the bedside of children who are often there for months on end. He and his wife and their two children, aged ten and five, live close to the Priory Green Estate in Islington, and first heard about the cooking classes for kids through their primary school.

"After work and school, you are so rushed as a family trying to get dinner on the table, but what we loved was the time to really learn how to cook with the kids and bond with them," he says. "It's a fantastic set-up, and the kids use real kitchen equipment. It's fairly safe with the chairs and worktops at a suitable height, but they are still cutting with knives, so they get a sense of responsibility. And now, as a result, they actually quite like cooking."

William and his wife, who also used to work in her Hong Kong-born parents' takeaway, usually cook Chinese food at home. They enjoyed widening their repertoire in the class and taking home what they had cooked. "We rarely got to eat what we helped to make in the takeaway unless someone had done the wrong order, so tasting what you have made and getting to take it home is really nice," he says.

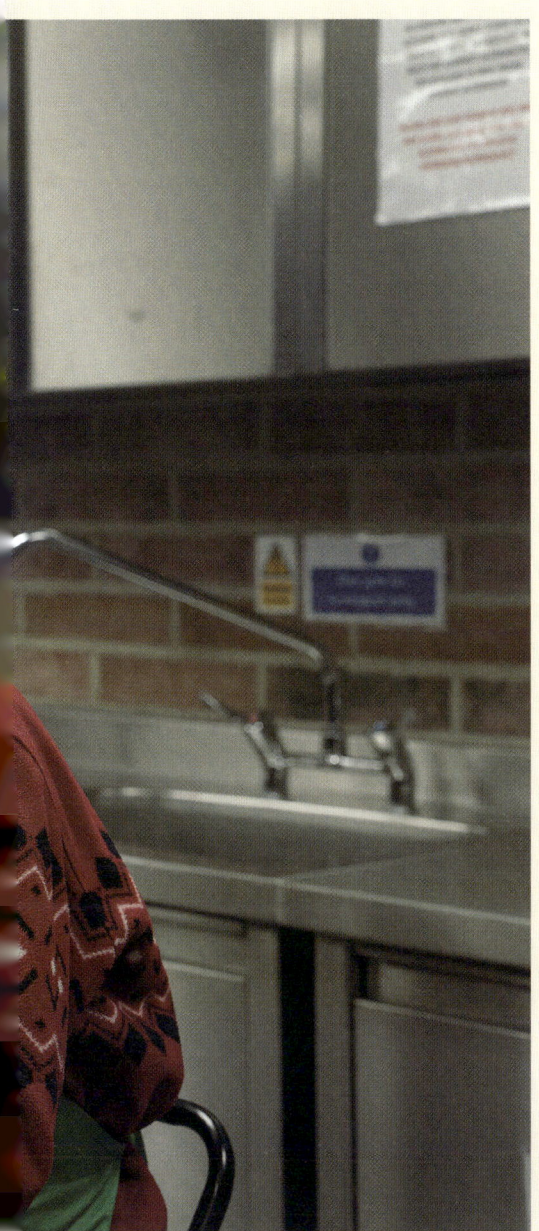

When the cost-of-living crisis hit, William and his family also joined the members using the Pantry on a Thursday. "It's really tough during a cost-of-living crisis when there isn't any support for people on a low income or single-income families," he says. "I suppose the idea of using a food bank has this kind of stigma attached to it, whereas at the Pantry there's less of that stigma because people are still paying for the produce," he says.

He says that there are often children in school uniform at the Pantry, reading, drawing, or chatting to other members. And he enjoys the human connection that comes with the "transaction" – there are no self-service checkouts at the Pantry.

"There's something quite nice about connecting with other humans who ask you how your week is and actually care about your answer, and who will give you the time to talk," he says.

William believes that as well as feeling connected to each other, members of the Pantry also feel more connected to the multinational companies whose vast glass and steel offices pepper the newer areas of King's Cross. "I think often there's this divide between the corporate world and the people who live near them," he says. "You might think it is us versus them, but actually these companies donate ingredients and equipment to the Pantry and even cook for the community too. It's lovely to know that they want to do that outreach and that they care as well."

It is this melting pot vibe that Cook for Good engenders that he appreciates the most. "I guess the working class can feel looked down upon in society, and likewise, if you're middle class, you might think people think you're pretentious or a bit snooty. But here, there is a real mix of people, and there is a mutual respect."

But it is the people of Cook for Good – the staff, the volunteers, the members – who truly make it special, he says. "It has a very friendly, positive vibe. Nothing feels like too big an ask, people are just happy to help – even though it's a very busy place. I think that's what makes it feel special; it restores your faith in humanity."

*Interview by Alexandra Topping*

**Prep time:**
15 minutes

**Resting time:**
30 minutes

**Cooking time:**
up to 1 hour

**Makes 12 balls**

# MATZO BALLS

Dumplings are a key element to so many traditional soups and there's no need to question why: they are simply pillows of joy that mop up all the brothy goodness. Matzo balls are a classic and one of our all-time favourites. We couldn't not include them, especially when we've got the perfect home for them: our traditional Jewish chicken soup goes to the next level when you add these.

## INGREDIENTS

**60g** matzo meal

**½ tsp** baking powder

**2** large eggs

**30ml** vegetable oil (or "schmaltz" – rendered or simulated chicken fat)

**2 litres** chicken stock (fresh, from **4** cubes, or just use salted water)

Optional spicing – a good pinch of any or all of ground ginger, garlic powder, onion powder

Salt – a good pinch

White pepper – a good pinch

## METHOD

Place the matzo meal, baking powder, salt, pepper, and whatever spices you are using (ginger, garlic, onion) into a medium bowl. Mix to combine. In a separate bowl, whisk the eggs and oil (or shmaltz) until very well combined and fluffy.

Pour the egg mixture into the dry ingredients. Mix all together with a fork until just combined – do not over-mix. Cover and put in the fridge to rest for 30 minutes (or overnight).

When ready to cook, put the stock or water into a large saucepan and bring to the boil over a medium heat. Shape the chilled mixture into 2.5cm balls (roughly walnut-sized) using damp hands to stop the mix sticking to them. Don't overwork, or they will end up very heavy.

Once the stock or water has come to the boil, reduce heat to a simmer. Drop the matzo balls gently into the liquid. Cover the pan and cook for 30–50 minutes, or until soft and fluffy. Keep the pan covered for at least the first 30 minutes.

When done, the balls should float on the surface and look light and tender. Slice one in half to test. They should look evenly cooked all the way through. If you see a darker or denser centre, simmer for longer.

Once cooked, transfer the matzo balls into your hot chicken soup to soak up the flavour, ready to serve. Or, if you want to prepare them in advance, just cook, cool, cover, and refrigerate until needed (for up to 72 hours). To freeze them, place the cooked, cooled balls in the freezer on a flat lined tray, then transfer to a sealed freezer container once frozen (after about 2 hours). Defrost at room temperature for an hour or in the fridge overnight, and then drop into hot soup, warm through, and serve.

**Prep time:**
15 minutes

**Cooking time:**
10 minutes

**Makes enough
for 20 servings**
(freezes well)

# GARLIC AND HERB CROUTONS

Making croutons is a brilliant way to use up stale loaves. You can use any leftover bread you have, even if just a half portion, and once made, the croutons keep for days. Though you might find they sometimes get eaten before the soup is ready.

## INGREDIENTS

**2** garlic cloves

**1 tbsp** dried mixed herbs

**1 × 400g** loaf bread
(sourdough if you have it)

**50g** unsalted butter

**20g** fresh parsley

**30ml** olive oil

**1½ tsp** freshly ground black pepper

**1½ tsp** sea salt flakes

## METHOD

Preheat the oven to 200°C/Gas mark 6. Line 2 baking sheets with non-stick baking paper.

Finely chop the garlic and parsley. Combine the olive oil, garlic, butter, herbs, dried herbs, salt, and pepper together in a very large bowl. Mix well.

Cut the bread into 2–3cm cubes. Add to the bowl with the butter mixture and fold through (using clean hands is best for this) to generously and evenly coat.

Spread the croutons out on 2 large baking sheets, making sure any leftover butter from the bowl goes onto the trays. Roast in the oven for 10 minutes until golden brown.

Remove from the oven and cool – you can crush them slightly for a crumblier texture.

**CHEF'S NOTE**     You can keep in an airtight container at room temperature for 5 days, or freeze and then just thaw and crisp up in the oven (or in a frying pan) when you want to use them. Allow the croutons to cool completely before storage.

# NO STRESS BREADS

We know that bread making can seem like a daunting task, requiring clever machines, aged starters, or well-honed skills, but it doesn't have to be that way. We have tried and tested all these in the Cook for Good Kitchen with cooks of all ages and skill levels, and we've never had a bad loaf yet. Whether you want a simple roll that allows the soup to shine, or a fancier focaccia loaded with treats, these recipes won't let you down.

**Prep time:**
15 minutes

**Resting time:**
45 minutes

**Cooking time:**
1 hour

**Makes 1 loaf**

# WHOLEGRAIN SEEDED LOAF

This wholesome loaf adds extra nourishment to any bowl of soup. It's particularly delicious with our carrot soup with orange and star anise or any other velvety, blended vegetable soup.

## INGREDIENTS

**400ml** warm water (approx. **40°C**)

**2 × 7g** packet instant/
fast action yeast

**2 tbsp** honey

**375g** strong wholemeal flour

**2 tbsp** wheat germ

**4 tbsp** digestive bran

**70g** sunflower seeds

**70g** pumpkin seeds

**1 tsp** salt

**3 tbsp** sunflower or rapeseed oil

**2 tbsp** sesame seeds

## METHOD

Lightly oil or butter a medium-to-large loaf tin or line with non-stick baking paper.

Pour 100ml of the water into a large mixing bowl. Add the yeast and honey. Mix and set in a warm place for 10 minutes or until frothy.

In separate mixing bowl, mix the flour, wheat germ, bran, sunflower and pumpkin seeds, and salt. When the yeast is frothy, add the dry ingredients to the yeast mix along with the oil and the remaining 300ml water. Mix thoroughly. The dough should be wet and sticky.

Spoon the dough into the prepared bread tin, sprinkle the sesame seeds on top, and place in a warm spot to prove for 40 minutes.

Preheat the oven to 180°C/Gas mark 4. Once hot, put the loaf in the oven to bake for 30 minutes. Reduce the heat to 160°C/Gas mark 3 and bake for another 30 minutes until cooked through. To test the doneness, insert a skewer into the centre of the loaf and it should come out clean; if not, bake a little longer (cover the top of the loaf with foil or non-stick baking paper if it's browning too much).

Turn out and cool for least 10 minutes on a wire rack before slicing.

**VARIATION**      You can substitute seeds with raisins if you prefer a sweeter, fruity option.

*See page 174 for wholegrain seeded loaf image*

# CORNBREAD

A classic pairing for Mexican-spiced soups like our Mexican chicken and black bean soup, but it's also delightful partnered with Karan Gokani's Sri Lankan curried butternut squash soup.

## INGREDIENTS

**115g** unsalted butter, plus extra to grease the tin

**2** eggs

**150g** sugar

**130ml** milk

**165ml** sour cream

**250g** plain flour

**125g** fine cornmeal

**¼ tsp** baking powder

**1 ½ tsp** bicarbonate of soda

**½ tsp** salt

## METHOD

Preheat the oven to 200°C/Gas mark 6. Generously coat a 12-cup muffin tin or small loaf tin with butter.

Melt the butter slowly in a small saucepan, being careful not to burn it, and set aside to cool. Whisk the eggs and sugar together in a large bowl until combined. Whisk the melted butter into the eggs. Add the sour cream and milk and whip until smooth.

Mix the cornmeal, flour, bicarbonate of soda, baking powder, and salt together in a large bowl. Gently fold the egg mixture into the flour mixture until just combined. Do not over-mix.

Use a large ice cream scoop or a measuring cup to divide the dough evenly among the muffin cups or pour the mix into your prepared loaf tin. Do not level or flatten the surface of the mounds.

Bake in the preheated oven until light golden brown and a toothpick inserted in the middle comes out with just a few crumbs attached, around 18 minutes for muffins or 25 minutes for a loaf.

Let the cornbread cool in the tin for 5 minutes and then flip out onto a wire rack to let cool for 10 minutes before serving. Serve warm with butter.

**Prep time:**
12 minutes

**Cooking time:**
30–50 minutes

**Makes 1 loaf or 8 rolls**

# CHEDDAR AND THYME SODA BREAD

Irish-style soda bread is one of the easiest breads you can make, as it doesn't require yeast or additional time to rise. The soda does all the magic, reacting with the acid from the buttermilk, yoghurt, or soured milk. This is a hearty loaf that's made for soup – we especially love it with our cream of spinach soup.

## INGREDIENTS

**100g** mature cheddar

**½ tbsp** thyme leaves

**250g** wholemeal flour

**100g** plain flour, plus
**25g** for dusting

**50g** porridge oats

**1 tsp** bicarbonate of soda

**1 tsp** salt

**1 tsp** honey or treacle

**1** large egg (optional, adds richness)

**300ml** buttermilk/full fat Greek yoghurt/full fat milk soured with
**1 tbsp** lemon juice or vinegar

## METHOD

Preheat the oven to 190ºC/Gas mark 5. Coarsely grate the cheddar. Strip the thyme leaves from the stalks and discard the stalks.

Place the flours, oats, bicarbonate of soda, 90g of the grated cheddar, thyme leaves, and salt in a bowl and mix. Reserve the rest of the cheese for sprinkling on top of the bread before baking.

In a separate bowl whisk together the buttermilk/yoghurt/soured milk, egg, and honey. Stir this mix into the flour mix using a fork.

When the dough starts to come together, use your hands to fully bring it into a round. Try not to overwork the dough. Lightly flour a baking sheet and place the round of dough on the sheet. Flatten it slightly into a disk of about 7cm thick. Cut a 3cm deep cross shape across the top of the dough with a large knife. Sprinkle the remaining cheese on top of the dough.

Bake for 30–40 minutes (in a fan oven) or up to 50 minutes (in a regular oven) or until a crust has formed on the top and the base sounds hollow when you tap it. Turn the finished bread onto a wire rack to cool. Serve warm with salted butter.

## VARIATIONS

### CHEESE, ONION, AND GARLIC SODA BREAD

Swap the thyme for 2 spring onions and 1 garlic clove. Clean, trim, and chop the spring onions. Peel and finely chop the garlic. Stir the chopped spring onions and garlic into the flour along with the cheddar.

### SODA BREAD ROLLS

To make rolls, follow the recipe until you have your round of dough on the baking sheet. Then split the dough equally into 8-10 rolls, flatten slightly, and cut a cross shape across the top of each with a blunt knife. The rolls should take around 20–25 minutes in the oven.

**Prep time:**
5 mins + 40 mins hydrating

**Resting time:**
1.5 hours

**Cooking time:**
25 minutes

**Makes 1 large loaf**

## INGREDIENTS

**550 g** water

**720 g** strong white bread flour, plus extra for dusting

**1 × 7 g** packet instant/fast action yeast

**2 tsp** salt

**1 tbsp** vegetable oil for greasing

# PORTUGUESE WATER BREAD

**This bread is as light as a cloud with a wonderful golden-brown crust. Perfect for sandwiches as it slices so well.**

## METHOD

Place the water and flour in the mixing bowl of a stand mixer and mix until fully incorporated. Leave to hydrate for 40 minutes.

Add the yeast and then knead on a medium speed with a dough hook for 10–12 minutes until the dough is elastic. Then, work the salt into the dough, giving it a final knead.

Lightly oil a large mixing bowl with any flavourless oil (e.g., vegetable oil, rapeseed oil). Transfer the dough to the oiled bowl and cover. Leave in a warm place to rest until doubled in size (approx. 1 ½ hours).

Towards the end of this time, preheat the oven to 250°C/Gas mark 9. Dust a baking tray with flour. If your oven doesn't go up to 250°C, then cook at 230°C/Gas mark 8 for an additional 10 minutes.

Transfer the dough to the prepared tray and then, without knocking out too much air, shape it into a loaf, tucking the sides of the dough underneath. You may find that oiling your hands makes this a little easier. Using a sharp knife, cut a slit length-ways along the top and then bake for 25–35 minutes until the loaf sounds hollow when tapped underneath.

Transfer to a wire rack to cool completely before serving.

# AMEL BENNACEUR

When Amel started volunteering at Cook for Good, she insisted that she do back-of-house jobs, like washing up. "I was quite shy," she says. "I preferred talking to the dishes."

She had been in the UK for several years, but a series of challenges had knocked her confidence. Amel was an English teacher in her home country of Algeria. She had studied hard and loved her job, but after getting married at the age of 22, she suffered domestic abuse at the hands of her husband and all she wanted to do was escape.

"I just wanted a place where I could be safe," she says. "After I arrived in the UK, I never wanted to leave again. I felt like no one could reach me easily here. It was a new life for me, a new start."

It was also the place where she found love and married again. "Things were not always easy, but it was so much better than what I had experienced before," she recalls. But when she got pregnant, she felt very isolated and lonely. A sufferer of acute asthma, she struggled with the pregnancy and ended up in intensive care. This was followed by a difficult birth which left her anxious and, with a new-born baby in her hands, sleep deprived. "I was like a zombie walking, and I became very anxious and nervous, but my husband did not give up on me."

Her health visitor helped her find her way back to better mental health by encouraging her to go to baby groups. At one of them, she got talking to an outreach worker from The Parent House, which led to her taking a parent mentoring course, and becoming a mentor for the charity. After having her second child, she decided to study for GSCEs in English, Maths, and Biology. "I got good grades," she says proudly. "I wanted my kids to see that their mummy could do something."

Amel had always loved baking and often took home-baked goods to The Parent House, so when she heard that Cook for Good were looking for volunteers, she decided to give it a try. "They were so welcoming straight away," she says. "I felt like I made lovely friends here, and now they are more than that – they are family. And the family is growing all the time."

The struggles in Amel's life are not over: her husband had an accident, had to quit work, and is now disabled; her son was diagnosed with ADHD and, during the pandemic, Amel, her husband, their two children, and her stepson were all sharing a one-bedroom flat. "It was very stressful," she explains. "I was always worried about my son." The family has been rehoused

but, despite looking after her husband, Amel does not receive a carer's allowance; while she has the right to remain in the UK, she has no recourse to public funds.

She explains that money is tight, but thanks to more training from Cook for Good she has been able to start working shifts, working in the kitchen for the organisation's corporate events. "It feels powerful earning my own money," she says. "I'd never been able to take my kids out to a restaurant because there was never enough money, but with that money we can eat out, I can take them to places."

After completing the Cook for Good Community Brigade training programme, Amel's confidence grew. She was encouraged to start performing front-of-house roles, welcoming guests, and going into companies to serve Cook for Good soup at lunchtimes. "It was so nice, they were so welcoming," she says. "They were normal people, just like us."

The front-of-house experience has brought her out of her shell. "Sometimes the guests ask about me and how I started working with Cook for Good, and it gives me more power, more confidence – I feel like I am not a lesser part of the community, I am a human being, and I can express myself."

In recent years, she has struggled with her own health and has been diagnosed with chronic fatigue syndrome. Nonetheless, Amel has her sights set firmly on the future. She loves to bake, and her ultimate goal is to open Amel's Café – a place where people of all ages can come and relax, have something delicious to eat, and share a few moments. "That's my dream," she says. "All children will be welcome, and there will be healthy food from different countries in the world – not just fish and chips!"

"But even if I don't get my business, I still feel human, I'm doing something I love, and I go home happy," she adds.

With every month that passes, she is moving closer towards that dream. At a recent event, when the guests finished eating, they applauded as Amel, who was serving as the assistant chef for the first time, came out of the kitchen. "It's a wonderful feeling," she says. "You feel like you are valued. Really, this place has given me my dream, it has given me life."

*Interview by Alexandra Topping*

# ROSEMARY AND GARLIC FOCACCIA

**Prep time:**
30 minutes

**Resting time:**
1.5 hours

**Cooking time:**
20–25 minutes

**Makes 1 large tray, enough for 12 portions**

What we love about this recipe is how easy it is to make. It's a wet dough that takes the shape of a roasting tray, which means you don't have to worry about shaping the loaf. Focaccia is also a versatile soup sponge with the delicious ability to soak up a myriad of global flavours.

## INGREDIENTS

**4** sprigs of rosemary

**1** garlic clove

**1 tbsp** (**15g**) fine salt

**625g** strong bread flour

**25g** coarse semolina

**1 × 7g** packet instant/ fast action yeast

**400ml** warm water (approx. **40°C**)

**80ml** olive oil

**1 tsp** sea salt flakes

**2 tsp** olive oil (for drizzling)

## METHOD

Reserve 1 sprig of rosemary for the garnish. Strip the leaves from the remaining 3 and finely chop. Peel and finely chop the garlic.

Put the salt, flour, semolina, and yeast into the mixer fitted with a dough hook (salt at the bottom, yeast at the top as they must NOT touch). Add the rosemary and garlic, warm water, and olive oil. Run the mixer until the ingredients form a dough – it will get less sticky as you work. Knead in the machine for 15–20 minutes (or you can knead by hand: tip the dough out onto a floured surface and knead for around 20 minutes until the dough is elastic).

Oil the sides and bottom of a large bowl. Transfer the dough to the oiled bowl, cover, and leave to prove in a warm place for 45 minutes or until roughly doubled in size.

Meanwhile, oil the bottom and sides of a 25×35cm roasting tray. Once dough has proved, place it on the roasting tray and gently spread out to fill the tray. Cover and prove for a second time in a warm place for 30 minutes.

Preheat the oven to 190°C/Gas mark 5. Cut the remaining rosemary sprigs into smaller sprigs. Uncover the dough and stretch out to fill the tray again. Poke your fingers into it to make "dimples" across the surface. Sprinkle with flaked sea salt, poke the small sprigs randomly into the top of the dough, and drizzle sparingly with olive oil.

Bake for 20–25 minutes – the bread should be lightly golden and cooked through. Allow to cool on a rack before serving. Serve with more olive oil to dip.

## VARIATIONS

### GREEN OLIVE AND ROSEMARY FOCACCIA

Strip the leaves from 3 sprigs of rosemary and finely chop them. Thinly slice 50g pitted green olives for the dough. Halve a further 50g pitted green olives for the top. Add the chopped rosemary and sliced olives when you add the water and olive oil to the flour mix. Cut 1 further sprig of rosemary into smaller sprigs.

Once the dough has proved in the roasting tray, sprinkle with 1 tsp sea salt flakes and then poke the small sprigs of rosemary and olive halves randomly into the top of the dough. Finish with 1 tsp olive oil. Bake as instructed in the main recipe.

### BLACK OLIVE AND CARAMELISED ONION FOCACCIA

Peel and finely slice 1 small red onion into half-moons. Finely chop 50g pitted black olives for the dough. Halve another 50g pitted black olives for the top. Add the chopped olives when you add the water and olive oil to the flour mix.

Set a frying pan over a medium heat. Add 2 tablespoons of olive oil followed by the sliced onion and a pinch of salt. Cook on a medium-high heat until starting to caramelise, stirring regularly, around 15–25 minutes. Once the onion is soft, add 1 tbsp brown sugar and mix well. Continue to cook until really caramelised and then set aside to cool.

Once the dough has proved in the roasting tray, sprinkle with 1 tsp sea salt flakes and then poke the olive halves into the top and scatter over the caramelised onion. Add a little more oil if needed (though the onion will provide a fair bit). Bake as instructed in the main recipe.

### SUNDRIED TOMATO AND FETA FOCACCIA

Cut 75g feta cheese into small 1cm cubes. Drain all the oil from 100g sundried tomatoes. Reserve the oil for the top (and/or to dip). Chop the sundried tomatoes into small pieces and add half when you add the water and olive oil to the flour mix.

Once the dough has proved in the roasting tray, sprinkle with 1 tsp sea salt flakes and then poke the feta cheese and remaining sundried tomatoes into the top of the dough. Drizzle sparingly with the reserved oil. Bake as instructed in the main recipe.

# CHALLAH

**Prep time:**
25 minutes

**Resting time:**
1 hour 45 minutes

**Cooking time:**
25–40 minutes

**Makes 1 loaf or 12 rolls**

Rich in flavour and steeped in history, challah is enriched with eggs and intertwined with symbolism. The braids are said to resemble interlocking arms, representing love, and the rounded loaves, with no beginning or end, to epitomise continuity. It's a gorgeous bread to share with a bowl of soup and is particularly lovely with our traditional Jewish chicken soup.

## INGREDIENTS

**3** eggs

**675g** plain flour

**250ml** warm water (approx. **40°C**)

**10g** salt

**30g** honey

**50ml** vegetable oil

**1 × 7g** packet instant/fast action yeast

**1 tbsp** sesame or poppy
seeds, to finish

## METHOD

Break the eggs into a large mixing bowl and whisk lightly with a fork. Put 2 tbsp of the egg mix aside in a small bowl for glazing the dough before baking.

Add the warm water, salt, honey, oil, yeast, and the whisked eggs. Give it a good mix to combine. Then, gradually add the flour, using a wooden spoon or your hands to work it in until it's fully incorporated. Knead for around 10 minutes until the dough is soft and smooth.

Place the dough in an oiled large bowl and cover. Leave in a warm place to rise for around 45 minutes or until roughly doubled in size. After this prove, punch back the dough.

### FOR CHALLAH ROLLS

Divide the dough into 12 equal parts and roll each one into a ball on a floured surface. Set the balls aside to rest for 5 minutes. Next, roll each ball and shape it into a long sausage-shaped cylinder around 15cm long. Starting with the first one, continue rolling the cylinders until they are around 28cm long. To shape into challah rolls, bend the length of dough into a U-shape and then cross one leg over the other. One leg gets tucked back up and in to the 'knot' and the other brought up and over the other side. Pinch the ends together to form the base of each roll.

### FOR A CHALLAH LOAF

Divide the dough into 4 equal parts and roll each into a ball on a floured surface. Set aside to rest for 5 minutes. Next, roll each ball into

lengths of 30cm and around 5cm wide. Put the 4 strands in a row, parallel to one another, and pinch the tops together.

If you're making this as a plaited loaf, there are lots of great videos online explaining how to do it.

Place the braided loaf or rolls on a lined baking sheet. Beat the remaining egg with a scant tablespoon of water (this is an egg wash) and brush it on to the dough. Cover lightly with cling film and let rise for another hour in a warm place until puffed up.

Preheat oven to 180°C/Gas mark 4. Brush the loaf or rolls again with egg wash. Sprinkle the dough with sesame or poppy seeds and then bake in the middle of the oven for 25–40 minutes or until golden. Rolls will take a shorter time to bake than loaves. Cool on a wire rack.

# EASY FLATBREADS

**Prep time:**
5 minutes

**Resting time:**
30 minutes

**Cooking time:**
15–20 minutes

**Makes 6 flatbreads**

We love pairing these flatbreads with hearty pulse-based bowls of nourishment, like our loved-by-all aromatic lentil soup or Dr Jane's lentil, tomato, and coconut dahl.

## INGREDIENTS

**115g** unsalted butter, plus extra to grease the tin

**2** eggs

**150g** sugar

**130ml** milk

**165ml** sour cream

**250g** plain flour

**125g** fine cornmeal

**¼ tsp** baking powder

**1 ½ tsp** bicarbonate of soda

**½ tsp** salt

## METHOD

Place the butter and milk in a small saucepan on a low heat until the butter is melted. Combine the flour with the salt in a large mixing bowl and then mix in the melted butter and milk until just incorporated. Use your hands to gently bring all the ingredients together; if the dough feels too wet, you can add a little more flour.

Transfer to a lightly floured surface and knead the dough for 3–5 minutes until the dough is smooth. Cover the dough and allow it to rest at room temperature for at least 30 minutes.

Dust the surface again with flour, then cut the dough into 6 even-sized pieces. Roll them into balls and then use a rolling pin to roll each into 20cm rounds (around 2.5mm thick).

Heat a frying pan on a high heat (dry) and then cook each flat bread for around 1 minute on each side until golden with little charred patches and slightly puffed. Turn to cook on the other side. Stack the cooked flatbreads on a plate and cover with a clean tea towel to keep them soft.

After cooking, eat warm and either plain or brushed with melted butter.

## AMEL'S MATLOU-A

**Prep time:**
5 minutes

**Resting time:**
30 minutes

**Cooking time:**
15–20 minutes

**Makes 6 flatbreads**

We were thrilled to get the recipe for this delicious semolina bread from Amel, one of our community volunteers. You can read her story on page 182.

## INGREDIENTS

**200ml** warm water (approx. **40°C**)

**1 × 7g** packet instant/
fast action yeast

**1½ tsp** caster sugar

**½ tsp** salt

**1 tsp** white distilled malt vinegar

**1 tbsp** olive oil, plus extra for oiling

**300g** plain white flour

**30g** fine semolina

## METHOD

Combine the warm water, yeast, and sugar in a large mixing bowl. Cover and put in a warm place or on top of a smaller bowl with some boiling water (make sure the boiling water doesn't touch the base of the bowl holding the yeast mix). Leave for 10 minutes until the yeast is activated; it should look a bit frothy.

Once activated, add in the salt, white vinegar, and olive oil. Mix well. Gradually whisk in the flour. Once the dough starts to come together, use your hands to fully incorporate all the ingredients and bring the dough together into a ball. Lightly oil a large bowl with a little olive oil and place the dough in the bowl. Cover and leave to prove in a warm place for around 45 minutes or until doubled in size.

Towards the end of the proving time, preheat the oven to 220°C/Gas mark 7. Set your oven to a no fan setting, just top and bottom heating. Put a baking sheet into the oven to preheat.

Next, lay out a sheet of non-stick baking paper on your counter-top and sprinkle it liberally with semolina. Knock back the dough slightly and then place it onto the paper. Shape the dough into a round of about 1cm thick and 20cm diameter, with rounded edges rather than straight sides. Sprinkle lightly with a little more semolina. Leave the dough to prove again for 15 minutes, lightly covered with a tea towel.

When ready to bake, remove the baking sheet from the oven and lift the baking paper with the dough straight onto the hot sheet. Bake for 15 minutes until the bread is golden and slightly risen. As soon as it's out of the oven, run a damp hand over the top of the bread and watch it transform into the softest bread.

# LEN KING AND
# DEL COOPER

There is a book written about the area where Len King (left) and Del Cooper (right) grew up. It's called Campbell Bunk: The Worst Street in London Between the Wars. Now 76 and 85, respectively, the pair grew up in a tumbledown four-bedroom house which was home to as many as 34 people from the same family line at any one time.

"There was a bowl on the floor of our bedroom to catch the rain," says Len. "My mum used to try and brush away the bed bugs. When people say, you know, when they were growing up, they had nothing as a youngster? Yeah, that was us, that was our generation. If we had a proper dinner once a year, that was a lot."

Len, who is Del's nephew, thinks he left school around the age of 14, and Del did the same, mainly because there was never enough money and there were a lot of mouths to feed. Often the many children living in the house went hungry. "When you got to 14, it was time to earn a shilling," says Len. "Since I was 14, I've never earned a fortune, but I've always kept my head above water."

The slum they lived in was eventually razed to the ground, and Len and Del moved on.

Throughout their childhood, kids, jobs, and marriages – and now in old age – they have been inseparable. "I owe him a fiver," jokes Del. "He's never going to let me forget it."

After Del married Marie, Len married her sister, Geraldine, and they became brothers-in-law too. The sisters were born in Ireland, but their parents had decided to emigrate when the Troubles started. "I was born in Derry; Marie was born in Limerick," says Geraldine. "But our parents couldn't get a house, couldn't get jobs because we were Catholics. So, we had to come to London."

After getting married, the two couples lived on the Priory Green Estate. They still live nearby, within striking distance of each other. "We loved living on the estate," says Del. "The kids all played together, and everyone looked out for each other. It had its problems, but we were happy there."

Sitting in Len and Geraldine's cosy and spotlessly clean living room, the kettle on the boil, a big plate of biscuits on the coffee table, Len and Del gently rib each other and finish each other's sentences. It is no surprise that when given the opportunity to get involved in the Men's Grub Club at Cook for Good, they did that together too.

Len lights up when he remembers how they got involved. The two couples were at the Pantry for the Good Neighbourhood Summer Fair Day, having a cup of tea, when Community Manager Martha Ahmet came over. "She said she didn't want to speak to the women, just the men," laughs Len.

After a bit of gentle persuasion, the pair signed up for the course, both admitting that cooking wasn't really their thing. Len had looked after his sons on his own for a while, but his cooking only stretched as far as sausages. In the Men's Grub Club, he learned how to cook healthier meals from scratch. "It was just really nice," says Len. "I liked the companionship of it." Del adds: "We didn't really know what to expect, but once we started, we just got into it. Everyone was friendly, everyone spoke to you, and you really learned how to cook."

Marie is definitely supportive of Del's newfound love of cooking. "He made me a lovely burger, all cooked from fresh – it was really nice!" she says, with just a hint of surprise.

All four of them go to the Pantry most weeks and love the community meals when everyone comes together. It reminds them of their younger years on the Priory Green Estate when everyone knew everyone. "It's so friendly, and we sit down and have a bit of a chat. I just like seeing everyone," says Len.

The four say that another highlight was a summer trip to Southend. "The coach was only £3," says Del. "It was scorching, and we got an ice cream. It was one of the best days."

But early in 2024, Len became seriously unwell and was diagnosed with a brain tumour. He went to the Pantry in late March for the first time in many weeks, and there was a queue of people saying hello and checking how he was doing. "I really want to get back there," he says. "I'm looking forward to spending time with people."

For Geraldine, who is looking after Len, the Pantry is also somewhere she can feel supported and have a break. "You can have a coffee, and if something's wrong, you can sit there and talk or just listen," she says.

*Despite his illness being at such an advanced stage, Len was determined to be part of Soup for Good; sadly, he passed away just a few weeks after this interview took place. He is much missed by the Priory Green community and the Cook for Good team, and we are grateful to his family for allowing us to share his story.*

*Interview by Alexandra Topping*

Leonard Edward King

26th September 1947
– 26th April 2024

# INDEX

## APPLE

Celeriac, kale, apple,
  and chilli soup. . . . . . . . . . . . . . 117
Curried parsnip soup . . . . . . . . . . 65

## ARTICHOKE

Mimi and Aya's pea and
  artichoke soup . . . . . . . . . . . . . . 69

## ASPARAGUS

Asparagus soup with
  lemon and Parmesan. . . . . . . . . 112
Ebrima's Gambian soup . . . . . . . . 111
Greek avgolemono soup. . . . . . . . 33

## BARLEY

Beef and barley soup . . . . . . . . . .155
Mixed vegetable soup . . . . . . . . . 86

## BEANS

Chicken and white bean soup
  with walnut pesto. . . . . . . . . . . 34
Greek avgolemono soup. . . . . . . . 33
Irma's minestrone . . . . . . . . . . . . .134
Mexican chicken and
  black bean soup . . . . . . . . . . . . 37
Sunday roast soup. . . . . . . . . . . . . 84
Tuscan bread soup. . . . . . . . . . . . 97

## BEANSPROUTS

Ed Balls' prawn pho . . . . . . . . . . .143

## BEETROOT

Ebrima's Gambian soup . . . . . . . . 111

## BEEF

Beef and barley soup . . . . . . . . . .155
Italian meatball,
  gnocchi, and kale soup . . . . . . .148
Mimi and Aya's pea and
  artichoke soup . . . . . . . . . . . . . 69
Sunday roast soup. . . . . . . . . . . . 84

## BREAD

Amel's matlou-a . . . . . . . . . . . . . .191
Black olive and
  caramelised onion focaccia . . . . .187
Challah . . . . . . . . . . . . . . . . . . . . .188
Cheddar and thyme soda bread . . .179
Cheese, onion, and
  garlic soda bread . . . . . . . . . . .179
Cornbread. . . . . . . . . . . . . . . . . . .177
Easy flatbreads . . . . . . . . . . . . . . .190
Garlic and herb croutons . . . . . . .173
Gazpacho . . . . . . . . . . . . . . . . . . .107
Green olive and
  rosemary focaccia. . . . . . . . . . .187

Italian meatball,
  gnocchi, and kale soup . . . . . . .148
Not-quite-French onion soup . . . .108
Portuguese water bread . . . . . . . .180
Roasted red pepper and fennel
  soup with wild garlic pesto . . . .123
Rosemary and garlic focaccia. . . . .187
Soda bread rolls. . . . . . . . . . . . . .179
Sundried tomato and
  feta focaccia. . . . . . . . . . . . . . .186
Tuscan bread soup. . . . . . . . . . . . 97
Wholegrain seeded loaf . . . . . . . .176

## BROCCOLI

Broccoli stalk soup. . . . . . . . . . . .101

## BUTTERNUT SQUASH

Butternut, sweet potato,
  and coconut soup . . . . . . . . . . . 48
Dr Jane's lentil, tomato,
  and coconut dahl . . . . . . . . . . . 75
Karan Gokani's Sri Lankan curried
  butternut squash soup . . . . . . . .133
Roasted butternut squash soup . . . 47
Tuscan bread soup. . . . . . . . . . . . 97

## CABBAGE

Greek avgolemono soup. . . . . . . . 33
Irma's minestrone . . . . . . . . . . . . .134
Sunday roast soup. . . . . . . . . . . . 84

## CARROT

Carrot soup with
  orange and star anise . . . . . . . . 115
Chicken and white bean soup
  with walnut pesto. . . . . . . . . . . 34
Emergency chicken noodle soup. . . 20
Homemade stock. . . . . . . . . . . . . .15
Italian meatball,
  gnocchi, and kale soup . . . . . . .148
Mimi and Aya's pea and
  artichoke soup . . . . . . . . . . . . . 69
Mixed vegetable soup . . . . . . . . . 86
Our Italian wedding soup. . . . . . . 27
Sunday roast soup. . . . . . . . . . . . 84
Thai chicken noodle soup. . . . . . . 24
Traditional Jewish
  chicken soup. . . . . . . . . . . . . . .18
Tuscan bread soup. . . . . . . . . . . . 97

## CAULIFLOWER

Cauliflower and coconut soup . . . . 53
Martha's favourite
  cauliflower cheese soup . . . . . . . 50

## CELERIAC

Celeriac, kale, apple,
  and chilli soup. . . . . . . . . . . . . . 117
Homemade stock. . . . . . . . . . . . .15

## CELERY

Broccoli stalk soup. . . . . . . . . . . .101
Emergency chicken noodle soup. . . 20
Mixed vegetable soup . . . . . . . . . 97
Sunday roast soup. . . . . . . . . . . . 84
Nigella's yellow split pea
  and frankfurter soup. . . . . . . . . .157

## CHEESE

Asparagus soup with
  lemon and parmesan. . . . . . . . . 112
Cheddar and thyme soda bread . . .179
Cheese, onion, and
  garlic soda bread . . . . . . . . . . .179
Chicken and white bean soup
  with walnut pesto. . . . . . . . . . . 34
Creamy parsnip and
  Parmesan soup . . . . . . . . . . . . . 63
Irma's minestrone . . . . . . . . . . . . .134
Italian meatball,
  gnocchi, and kale soup . . . . . . .148
Martha's favourite
  cauliflower cheese soup . . . . . . . 50
Mushroom and wild rice soup. . . . . 78
Not-quite-French onion soup . . . .108
Pea, mint and feta soup . . . . . . . . 66
Pesto. . . . . . . . . . . . . . . . . . . . . . .163
Roasted red pepper and fennel
  soup with wild garlic pesto . . . .123
Sundried tomato and
  feta focaccia. . . . . . . . . . . . . . .186
Tuscan bread soup. . . . . . . . . . . . 97

## CHICKEN

Chicken and white bean soup
  with walnut pesto. . . . . . . . . . . 34
Chinese-style chicken
  and sweetcorn soup . . . . . . . . . 23
Emergency chicken noodle soup. . . 20
Greek avgolemono soup. . . . . . . . 33
Homemade stock. . . . . . . . . . . . .15
Mexican chicken and
  black bean soup . . . . . . . . . . . . 37
Our Italian wedding soup. . . . . . . 27
Thai chicken noodle soup. . . . . . . 24
Traditional Jewish
  chicken soup. . . . . . . . . . . . . . .18
West African chicken
  and peanut soup. . . . . . . . . . . . 43

## CHICKPEAS

Fragrant chickpea soup
  with seeded garnish . . . . . . . . . .129
Rhimou's fast-breaking
  lamb harira soup. . . . . . . . . . . . .158

## CHILLI

Butternut, sweet potato,
  and coconut soup . . . . . . . . . . . 48
Celeriac, kale, apple,
  and chilli soup. . . . . . . . . . . . . . 117

Dr Jane's lentil, tomato,
and coconut dahl . . . . . . . . . . . 75
Ed Balls' prawn pho . . . . . . . . . . .143
Karan Gokani's Sri Lankan curried
butternut squash soup . . . . . . . .133
Loved-by-all
aromatic lentil soup . . . . . . . . . . 77
Mexican chicken and
black bean soup . . . . . . . . . . . . . 37
Mexican sweetcorn soup . . . . . . . 93
Thai chicken noodle soup . . . . . . . 24
Tomato salsa . . . . . . . . . . . . . . . .163
Tuscan bread soup . . . . . . . . . . . . 97
Wichet Khongphoon's
tom yum soup . . . . . . . . . . . . . .147

## COCONUT

Butternut, sweet potato,
and coconut soup . . . . . . . . . . . 48
Cauliflower and coconut soup . . . . 53
Curried parsnip soup . . . . . . . . . . 65
Dr Jane's lentil, tomato,
and coconut dahl . . . . . . . . . . . 75
Ebrima's Gambian soup . . . . . . . . 111
Loved-by-all
aromatic lentil soup . . . . . . . . . . 77
Mixed vegetable soup . . . . . . . . . 86
Thai chicken noodle soup . . . . . . . 24
Wichet Khongphoon's
tom yum soup . . . . . . . . . . . . . .147

## CORIANDER

Carrot soup with
orange and star anise . . . . . . . . 115
Curried parsnip soup . . . . . . . . . . 65
Ed Balls' prawn pho . . . . . . . . . . .143
Green goddess soup . . . . . . . . . . . 98
Mexican chicken and
black bean soup . . . . . . . . . . . . . 37
Mimi and Aya's pea and
artichoke soup . . . . . . . . . . . . . 69
Rhimou's fast-breaking
lamb harira soup . . . . . . . . . . . .158
Thai chicken noodle soup . . . . . . . 24
The Pantry's original tomato
and red lentil soup . . . . . . . . . . 57
Wichet Khongphoon's
tom yum soup . . . . . . . . . . . . . .147

## COURGETTE

Ebrima's Gambian soup . . . . . . . . 111
Fragrant chickpea soup
with seeded garnish . . . . . . . . . .129
Greek avgolemono soup . . . . . . . . 33
Irma's minestrone . . . . . . . . . . . .134

## CREAM

Broccoli stalk soup . . . . . . . . . . . .101
Cauliflower and coconut soup . . . . 53
Cream of mushroom soup . . . . . . .81
Cream of spinach soup . . . . . . . . . 94

Creamy parsnip and
Parmesan soup . . . . . . . . . . . . . 63
Fish pie soup . . . . . . . . . . . . . . . .140
Green goddess soup . . . . . . . . . . . 98
Herb-infused cream . . . . . . . . . . .165
Martha's favourite
cauliflower cheese soup . . . . . . 50
Mixed vegetable soup . . . . . . . . . 86
Mushroom and wild rice soup . . . . 78
Pea, mint, and feta soup . . . . . . . . 66

## CUCUMBER

Gazpacho . . . . . . . . . . . . . . . . . .107

## CURRY PASTE

Thai chicken noodle soup . . . . . . . 24

## CURRY POWER

Curried parsnip soup . . . . . . . . . . 65
Dr Jane's lentil, tomato,
and coconut dahl . . . . . . . . . . . 75
Karan Gokani's Sri Lankan curried
butternut squash soup . . . . . . . .133

## DILL

Our Italian wedding soup . . . . . . . 27
Roasted red pepper and fennel
soup with wild garlic pesto . . . . .123
Traditional Jewish
chicken soup . . . . . . . . . . . . . . .18

## EGGS

Challah . . . . . . . . . . . . . . . . . . . .188
Chinese-style chicken
and sweetcorn soup . . . . . . . . . 23
Cornbread . . . . . . . . . . . . . . . . . .177
Gazpacho . . . . . . . . . . . . . . . . . .107
Greek avgolemono soup . . . . . . . . 33
Italian meatball,
gnocchi, and kale soup . . . . . . .148
Matzo balls . . . . . . . . . . . . . . . . .170
Mimi and Aya's pea and
artichoke soup . . . . . . . . . . . . . 69
Our Italian wedding soup . . . . . . . 27

## FENNEL

Fennel and potato soup . . . . . . . .124
Greek avgolemono soup . . . . . . . . 33
Green goddess soup . . . . . . . . . . . 98
Homemade stock . . . . . . . . . . . . .15
Roasted red pepper and fennel
soup with wild garlic pesto . . . . .123

## FETA

Mexican sweetcorn soup . . . . . . . 93
Pea, mint, and feta soup . . . . . . . . 66
Sundried tomato and
feta focaccia . . . . . . . . . . . . . . .186

## FISH

Ed Balls' prawn pho . . . . . . . . . . .143
Fish pie soup . . . . . . . . . . . . . . . .140

Wichet Khongphoon's
tom yum soup . . . . . . . . . . . . . .147

## FRANKFURTER

Nigella's yellow split pea
and frankfurter soup . . . . . . . . .157

## GARLIC

Cheese, onion, and
garlic soda bread . . . . . . . . . . . .179
Chicken and white bean soup
with walnut pesto . . . . . . . . . . . 34
Chinese-style chicken
and sweetcorn soup . . . . . . . . . 23
Cream of mushroom soup . . . . . . .81
Cream of spinach soup . . . . . . . . . 94
Curried parsnip soup . . . . . . . . . . 65
Garlic and herb croutons . . . . . . .173
Gazpacho . . . . . . . . . . . . . . . . . .107
Gordon Brown's
real tomato soup . . . . . . . . . . . 54
Greek avgolemono soup . . . . . . . . 33
Green goddess soup . . . . . . . . . . . 98
Gremolata . . . . . . . . . . . . . . . . . .163
Homemade stock . . . . . . . . . . . . .15
Italian meatball,
gnocchi, and kale soup . . . . . . .148
Mimi and Aya's pea and
artichoke soup . . . . . . . . . . . . . 69
Mushroom and wild rice soup . . . . 78
Our Italian wedding soup . . . . . . . 27
Pesto . . . . . . . . . . . . . . . . . . . . . .163
Roasted red pepper and fennel
soup with wild garlic pesto . . . . .123
Rosemary and garlic focaccia . . . . .187
Thai chicken noodle soup . . . . . . . 24

## GREEN PEPPER

Gazpacho . . . . . . . . . . . . . . . . . .107

## GINGER

Butternut, sweet potato,
and coconut soup . . . . . . . . . . . 48
Chinese-style chicken
and sweetcorn soup . . . . . . . . . 23
Curried parsnip soup . . . . . . . . . . 65
Dr Jane's lentil, tomato,
and coconut dahl . . . . . . . . . . . 75
Ed Balls' prawn pho . . . . . . . . . . .143
Emergency chicken noodle soup. . . 20
Karan Gokani's Sri Lankan curried
butternut squash soup . . . . . . . .133
Loved-by-all
aromatic lentil soup . . . . . . . . . . 77
Mimi and Aya's pea and
artichoke soup . . . . . . . . . . . . . 69
Rhimou's fast-breaking
lamb harira soup . . . . . . . . . . . .158
West African peanut
and chicken soup . . . . . . . . . . . 43
Wichet Khongphoon's
tom yum soup . . . . . . . . . . . . . .147

## GNOCCHI

Italian meatball,
gnocchi, and kale soup . . . . . . .148

## KALE

Celeriac, kale, apple,
and chilli soup. . . . . . . . . . . . .117
Greek avgolemono soup. . . . . . . 33
Green goddess soup. . . . . . . . . . 98
Irma's minestrone . . . . . . . . . . .134
Italian meatball,
gnocchi, and kale soup . . . . . . .148
Tuscan bread soup. . . . . . . . . . . 97

## LAMB

Mimi and Aya's pea and
artichoke soup . . . . . . . . . . . . 69
Rhimou's fast-breaking
lamb harira soup. . . . . . . . . . . .158
Sunday roast soup . . . . . . . . . . . 84

## LEEK

Broccoli stalk soup. . . . . . . . . . .101
Beef and barley soup . . . . . . . . .155
Fish pie soup . . . . . . . . . . . . . . .140
Greek avgolemono soup. . . . . . . 33
Green goddess soup. . . . . . . . . . 98
Homemade stock. . . . . . . . . . . . .15
Martha's favourite
cauliflower cheese soup . . . . . . 50
Roasted butternut squash soup . . . 47
Traditional Jewish
chicken soup. . . . . . . . . . . . . . .18
Tuscan bread soup. . . . . . . . . . . 97

## LEMON

Asparagus soup with
lemon and Parmesan. . . . . . . . . 112
Ayse and Sue's Turkish red lentil
soup (mercimek corbasi). . . . . . .130
Broccoli stalk soup. . . . . . . . . . .101
Chicken and white bean soup
with walnut pesto. . . . . . . . . . . 34
Dr Jane's lentil, tomato,
and coconut dahl . . . . . . . . . . . 75
Greek avgolemono soup. . . . . . . 33
Gremolata. . . . . . . . . . . . . . . . .163
Pesto. . . . . . . . . . . . . . . . . . . . .163
Rhimou's fast-breaking
lamb harira soup. . . . . . . . . . . .158

## LEMONGRASS

Ed Balls' prawn pho . . . . . . . . . .143
Emergency chicken noodle soup . . 20
Wichet Khongphoon's
tom yum soup. . . . . . . . . . . . . .147

## LENTILS

Ayse and Sue's Turkish red lentil
soup (mercimek corbasi). . . . . . .130
Dr Jane's lentil, tomato,
and coconut dahl . . . . . . . . . . . 75
Fragrant chickpea soup
with seeded garnish . . . . . . . . .129
Mixed vegetable soup . . . . . . . . 86
Rhimou's fast-breaking
lamb harira soup. . . . . . . . . . . .158
The Pantry's original tomato
and red lentil soup . . . . . . . . . . 57

## LIME

Mexican Sweetcorn soup. . . . . . . 93
Thai chicken noodle soup. . . . . . . 24
Ed Balls' prawn pho . . . . . . . . . .143
Wichet Khongphoon's
tom yum soup. . . . . . . . . . . . . .147

## MEATBALLS

Italian meatball,
gnocchi, and kale soup . . . . . . .148
Our Italian wedding soup . . . . . . . 27

## MINT

Ayse and Sue's Turkish red lentil
soup (mercimek corbasi). . . . . . .130
Ed Balls' prawn pho . . . . . . . . . .143
Pea, mint, and feta soup. . . . . . . 66

## MUSHROOM

Cream of mushroom soup . . . . . . .81
Mushroom and wild rice soup. . . . 78
Wichet Khongphoon's
tom yum soup. . . . . . . . . . . . . .147

## NOODLES

Ed Balls' prawn pho . . . . . . . . . .143
Emergency chicken noodle soup. . . 20
Thai chicken noodle soup. . . . . . . 24

## OLIVE

Black olive and
caramelised onion focaccia . . . . .187
Gazpacho . . . . . . . . . . . . . . . . .107
Green olive and
rosemary focaccia. . . . . . . . . . .187

## ONION

Black olive and
caramelised onion focaccia . . . . .187
Callaloo soup. . . . . . . . . . . . . . .144
Crispy onions. . . . . . . . . . . . . . . 171
Gazpacho . . . . . . . . . . . . . . . . .107
Gordon Brown's
real tomato soup . . . . . . . . . . . 54
Homemade stock. . . . . . . . . . . . .15
Not-quite-French onion soup . . . .108
Sunday roast soup . . . . . . . . . . . 84
Tuscan bread soup. . . . . . . . . . . 97

## ORANGE

Carrot soup with
orange and star anise . . . . . . . . 115

## PARMESAN

Asparagus soup with
lemon and Parmesan. . . . . . . . . 112
Chicken and white bean soup
with walnut pesto. . . . . . . . . . . 34
Creamy parsnip and
Parmesan soup . . . . . . . . . . . . . 63
Irma's minestrone . . . . . . . . . . .134
Italian meatball,
gnocchi, and kale soup . . . . . . .148
Mushroom and wild rice soup. . . . 78
Our Italian wedding soup . . . . . . . 27
Pesto. . . . . . . . . . . . . . . . . . . . .163
Roasted red pepper and fennel
soup with wild garlic pesto . . . . .123
Tuscan bread soup. . . . . . . . . . . 97

## PARSLEY

Ayse and Sue's Turkish red lentil
soup (mercimek corbasi). . . . . . .130
Celeriac, kale, apple,
and chilli soup. . . . . . . . . . . . . 117
Chicken and white bean soup
with walnut pesto. . . . . . . . . . . 34
Fish pie soup . . . . . . . . . . . . . . .140
Fragrant chickpea soup
with seeded garnish . . . . . . . . .129
Garlic and herb croutons . . . . . . .173
Greek avgolemono soup. . . . . . . 33
Gremolata. . . . . . . . . . . . . . . . .163
Herb-infused cream. . . . . . . . . . .165
Herb oil . . . . . . . . . . . . . . . . . . .165
Homemade stock. . . . . . . . . . . . .15
Irma's minestrone . . . . . . . . . . .134
Italian meatball,
gnocchi, and kale soup . . . . . . .148
Mimi and Aya's pea and
artichoke soup . . . . . . . . . . . . 69
Mushroom and wild rice soup. . . . 78
Not-quite-French onion soup . . . .108
Our Italian wedding soup . . . . . . . 27
Rhimou's fast-breaking
lamb harira soup. . . . . . . . . . . .158
Tuscan bread soup. . . . . . . . . . . 97

## PARSNIP

Creamy parsnip and
Parmesan soup . . . . . . . . . . . . . 63
Curried parsnip soup . . . . . . . . . . 65
Homemade stock. . . . . . . . . . . . .15

## PASTA

Cream of mushroom soup . . . . . . .81
Irma's minestrone . . . . . . . . . . .134
Mixed vegetable soup . . . . . . . . 86
Our Italian wedding soup . . . . . . . 27
Pesto. . . . . . . . . . . . . . . . . . . . .163

## PEA

Fish pie soup . . . . . . . . . . . . . . .140
Greek avgolemono soup. . . . . . . . 33
Green goddess soup. . . . . . . . . . . 98
Mimi and Aya's pea and
   artichoke soup . . . . . . . . . . . . . 69
Nigella's yellow split pea
   and frankfurter soup. . . . . . . . .157
Pea, mint, and feta soup. . . . . . . . 66
Sunday roast soup. . . . . . . . . . . . 84

## PEANUT

Pesto. . . . . . . . . . . . . . . . . . . . .163
West African peanut
   and chicken soup . . . . . . . . . . . 43

## PESTO

Chicken and white bean soup
   with walnut pesto. . . . . . . . . . . 34
Pesto. . . . . . . . . . . . . . . . . . . . .163
Roasted red pepper and fennel
   soup with wild garlic pesto . . . .123

## PECORINO

Asparagus soup with
   lemon and Parmesan. . . . . . . . . 112
Chicken and white bean soup
   with walnut pesto. . . . . . . . . . . 34
Creamy parsnip and
   Parmesan soup . . . . . . . . . . . . . 63
Irma's minestrone . . . . . . . . . . . .134
Italian meatball,
   gnocchi, and kale soup . . . . . . .148
Mushroom and wild rice soup. . . . 78
Our Italian wedding soup . . . . . . . 27
Pesto. . . . . . . . . . . . . . . . . . . . .163
Roasted red pepper and fennel
   soup with wild garlic pesto . . . .123
Tuscan bread soup. . . . . . . . . . . . 97

## PLANTAIN

Ebrima's Gambian soup . . . . . . . . 111

## POTATO

Ayse and Sue's Turkish red lentil
   soup (mercimek corbasi). . . . . . .130
Beef and barley soup . . . . . . . . . .155
Broccoli stalk soup. . . . . . . . . . . .101
Cream of spinach soup. . . . . . . . . 94
Fennel and potato soup . . . . . . . .124
Fish pie soup . . . . . . . . . . . . . . .140
Green goddess soup. . . . . . . . . . . 98
Mexican sweetcorn soup . . . . . . . 93
Mimi and Aya's pea and
   artichoke soup . . . . . . . . . . . . . 69
Pea, mint, and feta soup. . . . . . . . 66
Sunday roast soup. . . . . . . . . . . . 84

## PRAWNS

Ed Balls' prawn pho . . . . . . . . . . .143
Wichet Khonghpoon's
   tom yum soup. . . . . . . . . . . . . .147

## RED PEPPER

Karan Gokani's Sri Lankan curried
   butternut squash soup . . . . . . . .133
Mexican chicken and
   black bean soup . . . . . . . . . . . . 37
Roasted red pepper and fennel
   soup with wild garlic pesto . . . .123
Thai chicken noodle soup . . . . . . . 24

## RICE

Greek avgolemono soup. . . . . . . . 33
Mixed vegetable soup . . . . . . . . . 86
Mushroom and wild rice soup. . . . 78
West African peanut
   and chicken soup . . . . . . . . . . . 43

## ROLLS

Challah . . . . . . . . . . . . . . . . . . . .188
Soda bread rolls. . . . . . . . . . . . . .179

## ROSEMARY

Green olive and
   rosemary focaccia. . . . . . . . . . .187
Rosemary and garlic focaccia. . . . .187
Sunday roast soup. . . . . . . . . . . . 84

## SAGE

Crispy sage . . . . . . . . . . . . . . . . .173

## SPINACH

Callaloo soup. . . . . . . . . . . . . . . .144
Chicken and white bean soup
   with walnut pesto. . . . . . . . . . . 34
Cream of spinach soup. . . . . . . . . 94
Greek avgolemono soup. . . . . . . . 33
Green goddess soup. . . . . . . . . . . 98
Irma's minestrone . . . . . . . . . . . .134
Pesto. . . . . . . . . . . . . . . . . . . . .163
West African peanut
   and chicken soup . . . . . . . . . . . 43

## SPRING ONION

Cheese, onion, and
   garlic soda bread . . . . . . . . . . .179
Chinese-style chicken
   and sweetcorn soup . . . . . . . . . 23
Greek avgolemono soup. . . . . . . . 33

## SWEETCORN

Chinese-style chicken
   and sweetcorn soup . . . . . . . . . 23
Homemade stock. . . . . . . . . . . . . .15
Irma's minestrone . . . . . . . . . . . .134
Mexican chicken and
   black bean soup . . . . . . . . . . . . 37
Mexican sweetcorn soup . . . . . . . 93

## SWEET POTATO

Butternut, sweet potato,
   and coconut soup . . . . . . . . . . . 48
Ebrima's Gambian soup . . . . . . . . 111
West African peanut
   and chicken soup . . . . . . . . . . . 43

## TARRAGON

Cream of mushroom soup . . . . . . .81
Herb-infused cream. . . . . . . . . . .165
Herb oils . . . . . . . . . . . . . . . . . . .165
Homemade stock. . . . . . . . . . . . . .15

## THYME

Callaloo soup. . . . . . . . . . . . . . . .144
Carrot soup with
   orange and star anise . . . . . . . . 115
Cheddar and thyme soda bread . . .179
Chicken and white bean soup
   with walnut pesto. . . . . . . . . . . 34
Fragrant chickpea soup
   with seeded garnish . . . . . . . . .129
Greek avgolemono soup . . . . . . . . 33
Not-quite-French onion soup . . . . .108
Sunday roast soup. . . . . . . . . . . . 84

## TOMATO

Dr Jane's lentil, tomato
   and coconut dahl . . . . . . . . . . . 75
Fragrant chickpea soup
   with seeded garnish . . . . . . . . .129
Gazpacho . . . . . . . . . . . . . . . . . .107
Gordon Brown's
   real tomato soup . . . . . . . . . . . 54
Irma's minestrone . . . . . . . . . . . .134
Loved-by-all
   aromatic lentil soup . . . . . . . . . 77
Mexican chicken and
   black bean soup . . . . . . . . . . . . 37
Rhimou's fast-breaking
   lamb harira soup. . . . . . . . . . . .158
Sundried tomato and
   feta focaccia. . . . . . . . . . . . . . .186
The Pantry's original tomato
   and red lentil soup . . . . . . . . . . 57
Tomato salsa. . . . . . . . . . . . . . . .163
Tuscan bread soup. . . . . . . . . . . . 97
Wichet Khonghpoon's
   tom yum soup. . . . . . . . . . . . . .147

## WALNUTS

Chicken and white bean soup
   with walnut pesto. . . . . . . . . . . 34

## WILD GARLIC

Greek avgolemono soup. . . . . . . . 33
Herb-infused cream. . . . . . . . . . .165
Herb oils . . . . . . . . . . . . . . . . . . .165
Roasted red pepper and fennel
   soup with wild garlic pesto . . . .123

# SOME VERY BIG THANK YOUS

Deciding to produce a book of recipes and stories with no publishing experience and little extra capacity in our day jobs might seem like a slightly crazy decision (and, at times, it definitely felt that way). But we have been fortunate enough to have support and goodwill from some incredible people who have known exactly what we needed to do, and how, and when. We are overwhelmed by how generously they have shared their opinions, expertise, and time.

Our first thank you must go to our four culinary impact partners: BaxterStorey, Genuine Dining, Houston & Hawkes, and Restaurant Associates. In the two years since we opened our kitchen, they have supported us in many ways, from lending us chefs for our community cooking classes to sharing ideas for future activities. And by covering the production costs of this book, they have ensured that 100% of the profits from every sale will be invested in our community programme.

Additional thanks must also go to Deloitte, Havas, Peabody, Phoenix Court Works, and TP Bennett, who have also lent us support with the production of this book. And on the subject of Peabody, it is important to note that we wouldn't have a pantry or a kitchen on the Priory Green Estate without them; they have leased us our spaces rent-free and been with us every step of the way. We must also thank

Food Bank Aid and The Felix Project for stocking the Pantry with ingredients for soup and many other meals each week, and Coverpoint Foodservice Consulting for their professional guidance on all things soup.

We are proud to be including recipes from some fantastic supporters. They have not only donated their favourite soup recipes but have also shared their time, energy, and creativity with us over the past few years: hosting Supper Clubs, delivering cooking courses, writing about us in the media, and surprising our members in the Pantry. Thank you to Ed Balls, Gordon and Sarah Brown, Karan Gokani, Wichet Khongphoon, and Dr Jane Myat. And an extra special thanks to Nigella Lawson for also writing such a generous foreword for this book.

As well as being a recipe book, *Soup for Good* is a piece of social history, featuring our community members' very personal lives. Knowing we needed people we could trust to tell their stories with respect and kindness, we turned to writer Lexy Topping and photographer Martin Godwin, who had visited our Pantry two years ago and produced a beautiful piece for us in The Guardian. They have once again captured the essence of these wonderful people, and done so in a way that made the experience enjoyable for everyone.

We are also hugely grateful to Nikki Littman and Manuel Harlan, who have helped us with copyediting and additional photography, respectively. Thanks, too, to Jo Burkill and Jim Glass for their generous advice and ideas and to Laura Creyke at Mark Hutchinson Management for helping us get the news about this book out there.

Keeping a project of this size on time and budget with a first-time team and so many complex strands is no mean feat; but our project manager, Louise Machin, has been on top of it all. Lou has been incredibly patient and calm, keeping us on track from project plan to final manuscript and ensuring all our plates stayed spinning.

Sometimes you don't know how much you need someone until you meet them and that was certainly the case when we had our first conversation with our culinary editor and food stylist, Rachel de Thample. It's fair to say that we all let out a huge sigh of relief when we realised we were in the hands of someone so experienced and so talented. Her insights and creativity have helped lift this book to a level of professionalism that we could not have managed alone.

We believe in keeping things in the family whenever we can so when it came to choosing a food photographer, there was really only one choice. Jason Boswell is a fantastic chef who has supported us at numerous corporate and community events. He also has a successful side hustle as an award-winning food photographer with his company, Stepstone Imaging. It's wonderful to see our favourite soups in gorgeous technicolour.

Similarly, Dan Reeves and Jodie Douglas from Reeves Creative may not technically be part of the Cook for Good team, but their visual skills and design expertise are behind everything we produce. So we went straight to them when we wanted to narrow down a visual route for our cover – and, as always, they overdelivered.

At the beginning of this journey, we sought advice from other people who had self-published, and Lexy Topping introduced us to Natasha Edwards, who runs the Garlic Farm on the Isle of Wight. This proved to be a pivotal conversation as Natasha not only gave us the confidence to go it alone, but also introduced us to Dan Jacobs at PrintHouse Corporation. Our first meeting with Dan left us in no doubt that he was the right person to take on *Soup for Good*. He and designer Aleksander Lenart have delivered a high-quality, stylish, and elegant book which is a joy to use and to read.

While it felt like a brave decision to self-publish our book, we were certainly not alone and have been aided by our friends at Curtis Brown agency, in particular Jonny Geller and Sabhbh Curran who provided a huge amount of wisdom along the way. We would undoubtedly have gone down several wrong turns without their help. A special thanks to Jonny (who just happens to be married to Karen) for spending many hours – at home and work – not only tasting our soups but adding some sage advice along the way.

The Cook for Good staff team is small but mighty: a group of colleagues who share our values, our love of soup, and our commitment to making life better for everyone. We are grateful every day to be working with Tom Kedge, Poornima Kirloskar-Sani, John Leach, Caroline Lisberg, Nicola Miller, and Zeina Nour. And we must give an extra shout out to a few members of the team who have been deeply involved in the creation of this book, all while juggling their day jobs.

Emma Stewart and Miriam Emanuel, our development director and partnerships manager, respectively, have done an excellent job of telling the story of this book to our clients and partners and bringing our wider sales strategy to life. Thanks to their efforts, we pre-sold over two thousand copies before the manuscript was even finalised.

Our resident chef, Simone Krieger, was tasked (at very short notice) with recipe testing and production for 50 soups and 24 breads and toppings in between hosting cooking events for corporate teams and community members. Simone approached this task, as she does everything, with grace, humour, and an extra helping of calm. She was ably assisted in this process by members of our Community Brigade, chefs Shane Pearson, Adam Phillips, and Keith Phillips, and our kitchen technician, Sue Benson, who made sure our kitchen was spotless and ready to go.

Martha Ahmet, our Community Manager, was our first Cook for Good hire. She has since spent three years building relationships with and between the members of our community. It is thanks to the trust they have in her that they trusted us to share their stories, and she worked closely with the members and with Lexy and Martin to make the process smooth and comfortable. She is the heart and face of Cook for Good for both our members and our volunteers.

There is one person who has been a constant throughout this project – from the moment it was just an idea until the final full stop when the manuscript went to print. Cathy Halstead is so much more than our comms manager; she is the custodian of all that is written by and about Cook for Good. She has brought the same qualities to the process that she brings to everything she does: talent, compassion, humour, and team spirit. She is a joy to work with, and we are so grateful for her incredible contribution to every aspect of this book.

Whenever we bring visitors to the Pantry, they always comment on how much they enjoyed meeting our community volunteers. This group of local residents, who give so generously of their time, are the power behind our organisation. They have helped turn a disused space into a place where everyone feels at home. They are patient, kind, and supportive, and we count ourselves extremely lucky to have them working with us.

Our 400 Pantry members are our closest allies and fiercest soup critics. They love to debate the virtues of chunky versus smooth and can be relied on to give us the frankest of feedback on anything we serve. It is thanks to them that we were able to create the list of favourites which we have shared with you between these pages.

And finally, we would like to thank the individuals who agreed to share their stories with us in this book: Ijeoma Anyanwu, Amel Bennaceu, Rhiz Chab, James Cope, Alec Erotokritou, Mary Harvey, Safia Hassan, Rebecca Henderson, William Lau, Esin Ozen, Nicolas Sinclair, and uncle and nephew, Del Cooper and Len King. Although we already knew quite a lot about their lives, we found these stories so moving and inspiring to read. We hope you do too.

With thanks to our culinary partners, who have funded the publication of *Soup for Good*, allowing us to invest all the profits into our community programme.

HOUSTON & HAWKES

RESTAURANT ASSOCIATES

Additional thanks to these partners for providing extra support for our book.

tp bennett